5

CONGRESSIONAL POLICIES, PRACTICES AND PROCEDURES

CONGRESSIONAL INVESTIGATIONS OF THE DEPARTMENT OF JUSTICE AND CLAIMS OF EXECUTIVE PRIVILEGE

CONGRESSIONAL POLICIES, PRACTICES AND PROCEDURES

Additional books in this series can be found on Nova's website under the Series tab.

Additional E-books in this series can be found on Nova's website under the E-book tab.

LAWS AND LEGISLATION

Additional books in this series can be found on Nova's website under the Series tab.

Additional E-books in this series can be found on Nova's website under the E-book tab.

CONGRESSIONAL POLICIES, PRACTICES AND PROCEDURES

CONGRESSIONAL INVESTIGATIONS OF THE DEPARTMENT OF JUSTICE AND CLAIMS OF EXECUTIVE PRIVILEGE

NATHAN DE VOS
EDITOR

New York

For permission to use material from this book please contact us:
Telephone 631-231-7269; Fax 631-231-8175
Web Site: http://www.novapublishers.com

Library of Congress Cataloging-in-Publication Data

ISBN: 978-1-62808-073-5

Published by Nova Science Publishers, Inc. †New York

CONTENTS

PREFACE

Legislative oversight is most commonly conducted through congressional budget, authorization, appropriations, confirmation, and investigative processes, and, in rare instances, through impeachment. But the adversarial, often confrontational, and sometimes high profile nature of congressional investigations sets it apart from the more routine, accommodative facets of the oversight process experienced in authorization, appropriations, or confirmation exercises. While all aspects of legislative oversight share the common goals of informing Congress so as to best accomplish its tasks of developing legislation, monitoring the implementation of public policy, and disclosing to the public how its government is performing, the inquisitorial process also sustains and vindicates Congress's role in our constitutional scheme of separated powers and checks and balances. The rich history of congressional investigations from the failed St. Clair expedition in 1792 through Teapot Dome, Watergate, Iran-Contra, Whitewater, and the current ongoing inquiries into Operation Fast and Furious, has established, in law and practice, the nature and contours of congressional prerogatives necessary to maintain the integrity of the legislative role in that constitutional scheme. This book reviews the legal basis for investigative oversight, followed by several prominent examples of congressional oversight that reflects the significant breadth and reach of the legislative investigative prerogative vis-a-vis the Department.

Chapter 1 – Legislative oversight is most commonly conducted through congressional budget, authorization, appropriations, confirmation, and investigative processes, and, in rare instances, through impeachment. But the adversarial, often confrontational, and sometimes high profile nature of congressional investigations sets it apart from the more routine, accommodative facets of the oversight process experienced in authorization, appropriations, or confirmation exercises. While all aspects of legislative oversight share the common goals of informing Congress so as to best accomplish its tasks of developing legislation, monitoring the implementation of public policy, and disclosing to the public how its government is performing, the inquisitorial process also sustains and vindicates Congress's role in our constitutional scheme of separated powers and checks and balances. The rich history of congressional investigations from the failed St. Clair expedition in 1792 through Teapot Dome, Watergate, Iran-Contra, Whitewater, and the current ongoing inquiries into Operation Fast and Furious, has established, in law and practice, the nature and contours of congressional prerogatives necessary to maintain the integrity of the legislative role in that constitutional scheme. A review of the historical experience pertinent to congressional access to information regarding the law enforcement activities of the Department of Justice indicates that the vast majority of requests for materials are resolved through political negotiation and accommodation, without the need for judicial resolution. Absent an executive privilege claim or a statute barring disclosure there appears to be no court precedent imposing a threshold burden on committees to demonstrate a "substantial reason to believe wrongdoing occurred" in order to obtain information. Instead, an inquiring committee need only show that the information sought is within the broad subject matter of its authorized jurisdiction, is in aid of a legitimate legislative function, and is pertinent to the area of concern. In the last 85 years, Congress has consistently sought and obtained access to information concerning prosecutorial misconduct by Department of Justice officials in closed cases; and access to pre-decisional deliberative prosecutorial memoranda—while often resisted by the Department—is usually released upon committee insistence as well. In contrast, the Department rarely releases—and committees rarely subpoena—material relevant to open criminal investigations. Typically, disputes are resolved without recourse to an executive privilege claim. Instead, negotiations produce various compromises: narrowing informational requests, delaying the release of information that could have prejudicial consequences on prosecutions, or redacting sensitive materials. However, when Presidents do claim executive privilege, courts have been reluctant to resolve the dispute. Indeed, litigation over the scope of executive privilege in direct relation to congressional oversight and investigations has been quite limited. In total, there have been four cases dealing with executive privilege in the context of information access disputes between Congress and the executive, and two of those resulted in decisions on the merits. The Supreme Court has never addressed executive privilege in the face of a congressional demand for information.

Chapter 2 – Presidential claims of a right to preserve the confidentiality of information and documents in the face of legislative demands have figured prominently, though intermittently, in executive-congressional relations since at least 1792. Few such interbranch disputes over access to information have reached the courts for substantive resolution. The vast majority of these disputes are resolved through political negotiation and accommodation. In fact, it was not until the Watergate-related lawsuits in the 1970's seeking access to President Nixon's tapes that the existence of a presidential confidentiality privilege was judicially established as a necessary derivative of the President's status in our constitutional scheme of separated powers. There have been only four cases involving information access disputes between Congress and the executive, and two of these resulted in decisions on the merits. The Nixon and post-Watergate cases established the broad contours of the presidential communications privilege. Under those precedents, the privilege, which is constitutionally rooted, could be invoked by the President when asked to produce documents or other materials or information that reflect presidential decision making and deliberations that he believes should remain confidential. If the President asserts the privilege, the materials become presumptively privileged. The privilege, however, is qualified, not absolute, and can be overcome by an adequate showing of need. Finally, while reviewing courts have expressed reluctance in balancing executive privilege claims against a congressional demand for information, they have acknowledged they will do so if the political branches have tried, in good faith, but failed to reach an accommodation. Until the District of Columbia Circuit's 1997 ruling in In re Sealed Case (Espy), and its 2004 decision in Judicial Watch v. Department of Justice, these earlier judicial decisions left considerable gaps in the law of presidential privilege. Among the more significant issues left open included whether the President has to have actually seen or been familiar with the disputed matter; whether the presidential privilege encompasses documents and information developed by, or in the possession of, officers and employees in the departments and agencies of the Executive Branch, outside of the Executive Office of the President; whether the privilege encompasses all communications with respect to which the President may be interested or is confined to presidential decision making and, if so, is limited to a particular type of presidential decision making; and precisely what kind of demonstration of need must be shown to overcome the privilege and compel disclosure of the materials. The unanimous panel in

Espy, and the subsequent reaffirmation of the Espy principles articulated in Judicial Watch, addressed each of these issues in a manner that may have drastically altered the future legal playing field in resolving such disputes. A more recent dispute with Congress involving the removal and replacement of nine United States Attorneys drew formal claims of privilege by President George W. Bush. Those privilege claims were challenged in a civil suit brought by the House Judiciary Committee seeking declaratory and injunctive relief with respect to refusals to appear, to testify, and to provide documents by two subpoenaed present and former officials. A district court decision on the merits, upholding the committee's challenge supplements the D.C. Circuit case law on this issue. President Obama formally invoked executive privilege for the first time on June 20, 2012, over documents sought by the House Committee on Oversight and Government Reform in its ongoing investigation into Operation Fast and Furious.

In: Congressional Investigations …
Editor: Nathan De Vos

ISBN: 978-1-62808-073-5

Chapter 1

CONGRESSIONAL INVESTIGATIONS OF THE DEPARTMENT OF JUSTICE, 1920-2012: HISTORY, LAW, AND PRACTICE*

Alissa M. Dolan and Todd Garvey

SUMMARY

Legislative oversight is most commonly conducted through congressional budget, authorization, appropriations, confirmation, and investigative processes, and, in rare instances, through impeachment. But the adversarial, often confrontational, and sometimes high profile nature of congressional investigations sets it apart from the more routine, accommodative facets of the oversight process experienced in authorization, appropriations, or confirmation exercises. While all aspects of legislative oversight share the common goals of informing Congress so as to best accomplish its tasks of developing legislation, monitoring the implementation of public policy, and disclosing to the public how its government is performing, the inquisitorial process also sustains and vindicates Congress's role in our constitutional scheme of separated powers and checks and balances. The rich history of congressional investigations from the failed St. Clair expedition in 1792 through Teapot Dome, Watergate, Iran-Contra, Whitewater, and the current ongoing

* This is an edited, reformatted and augmented version of a Congressional Research Service publication, CRS Report for Congress R42811, prepared for Members and Committees of Congress, from www.crs.gov, dated November 5, 2012.

inquiries into Operation Fast and Furious, has established, in law and practice, the nature and contours of congressional prerogatives necessary to maintain the integrity of the legislative role in that constitutional scheme.

A review of the historical experience pertinent to congressional access to information regarding the law enforcement activities of the Department of Justice indicates that the vast majority of requests for materials are resolved through political negotiation and accommodation, without the need for judicial resolution. Absent an executive privilege claim or a statute barring disclosure there appears to be no court precedent imposing a threshold burden on committees to demonstrate a "substantial reason to believe wrongdoing occurred" in order to obtain information. Instead, an inquiring committee need only show that the information sought is within the broad subject matter of its authorized jurisdiction, is in aid of a legitimate legislative function, and is pertinent to the area of concern. In the last 85 years, Congress has consistently sought and obtained access to information concerning prosecutorial misconduct by Department of Justice officials in closed cases; and access to pre-decisional deliberative prosecutorial memoranda—while often resisted by the Department—is usually released upon committee insistence as well. In contrast, the Department rarely releases—and committees rarely subpoena—material relevant to open criminal investigations. Typically, disputes are resolved without recourse to an executive privilege claim. Instead, negotiations produce various compromises: narrowing informational requests, delaying the release of information that could have prejudicial consequences on prosecutions, or redacting sensitive materials. However, when Presidents do claim executive privilege, courts have been reluctant to resolve the dispute. Indeed, litigation over the scope of executive privilege in direct relation to congressional oversight and investigations has been quite limited. In total, there have been four cases dealing with executive privilege in the context of information access disputes between Congress and the executive, and two of those resulted in decisions on the merits. The Supreme Court has never addressed executive privilege in the face of a congressional demand for information.

INTRODUCTION

Throughout its history, Congress has engaged in oversight of the executive branch—the review, monitoring, and supervision of the implementation of public policy. The first several Congresses inaugurated such important oversight techniques as special investigations, reporting requirements, resolutions of inquiry, and use of the appropriations process to review executive activity. Contemporary developments, moreover, have increased the legislature's capacity and capabilities to check on and check the executive. Public laws and congressional rules have measurably enhanced Congress's implied power under the Constitution to conduct oversight.[1]

Congressional oversight of the executive is designed to fulfill a number of important purposes and goals: to ensure executive compliance with legislative intent; to improve the efficiency, effectiveness, and economy of governmental operations; to evaluate program performance; to prevent executive encroachment on legislative powers and prerogatives; to investigate alleged instances of poor administration, arbitrary and capricious behavior, abuse, waste, fraud, and dishonesty; to assess agency or officials' ability to manage and carry out program objectives; to assess the need for new federal legislation; to review and determine federal financial priorities; to protect individual rights and liberties; and to inform the public as to the manner in which its government is performing its public duties, among others.[2]

Legislative oversight is most commonly conducted through congressional budget, authorization, appropriations, confirmation, and investigative processes, and, in rare instances, through impeachment. But the adversarial, often confrontational, and sometimes high profile nature of congressional investigations sets it apart from the more routine, accommodative facets of the oversight process experienced in authorization, appropriations, or confirmation exercises. While all aspects of legislative oversight share the common goals of informing Congress so as to best accomplish its tasks of developing legislation, monitoring the implementation of public policy, and of disclosing to the public how its government is performing, the inquisitorial process also sustains and vindicates Congress's role in our constitutional scheme of separated powers and checks and balances. The rich history of congressional investigations from the failed St. Clair expedition in 1792 through Teapot Dome, Watergate, Iran-Contra, Whitewater, and the current ongoing inquiries into Operation Fast and Furious, has established, in law and practice, the nature and contours of congressional prerogatives necessary to maintain the integrity of the legislative role in that constitutional scheme.

Congress's power of inquiry extends to all executive departments, agencies, and establishments in equal measure. Over time, however, congressional probes of the Department of Justice (Department or DOJ) have proved to be amongst the most contentious, stemming from the presumptive sensitivity of its principal law enforcement mission. Often, inquiries have been met with claims of improper political interference with discretionary deliberative prosecutorial processes, accompanied by refusals to supply internal documents or testimony sought by jurisdictional committees, based on assertions of constitutional and common law privileges or general statutory exemptions from disclosure. But the notion of, and need for, protection of the internal deliberative processes of agency policymaking, heightened sensitivity to premature disclosures of decision making involving law enforcement investigations, civil and criminal prosecutions, or security matters, is not unique to the DOJ, though the degree of day-to-day involvement there with such matters may be greater. An in-depth examination of the nature, scope, and resolution of such past investigative confrontations with the DOJ appears useful for informing future committees determining whether to undertake similar probes of DOJ, or other executive agencies, as to the scope and limits of their investigative prerogatives and the practical problems of such undertakings.

A review of the historical experience pertinent to congressional access to information regarding the law enforcement activities of the Department of Justice indicates that the vast majority of requests for materials are resolved through political negotiation and accommodation, without the need for judicial resolution. Absent an executive privilege claim or a statute barring disclosure there appears to be no court precedent imposing a threshold burden on committees to demonstrate a "substantial reason to believe wrongdoing occurred" in order to obtain information. Instead, an inquiring committee need only show that the information sought is within the broad subject matter of its authorized jurisdiction, is in aid of a legitimate legislative function, and is pertinent to the area of concern. In the last 85 years, Congress has consistently sought and obtained access to information concerning prosecutorial misconduct by Department of Justice officials in closed cases; and access to pre-decisional deliberative prosecutorial memoranda—while often resisted by the Department—is usually released upon committee insistence, as well. In contrast, the Department rarely releases—and committees rarely subpoena—material relevant to open criminal investigations.[3] Typically, disputes are resolved without recourse to an executive privilege claim. Instead, negotiations produce various compromises: narrowing informational requests, delaying the release of information that could have prejudicial consequences on prosecutions, or redacting sensitive materials.[4] However, when Presidents do claim executive privilege, courts have been reluctant to resolve the dispute. Indeed, litigation over the scope of executive privilege in direct relation to congressional oversight and investigations has been quite limited. In total, there have been four cases dealing with executive privilege in the context of information access disputes between Congress and the executive,[5] and two of those resulted in decisions on the merits.[6] The Supreme Court has never addressed executive privilege in the face of a congressional demand for information.

Committees, however, normally have been restrained by prudential considerations that involve a pragmatic assessment of the costs and benefits of demanding disclosure of information. Committees often weigh the legislative need, public policy, and their statutory duty to engage in continuous oversight of the application, administration, and execution of laws that fall within their jurisdiction against the potential burdens and harms to an agency if deliberative process matters are publically disclosed. In particular, sensitive law enforcement concerns and duties of the Justice Department have been seen to merit that substantial weight be given the agency's deliberative processes in the absence of a committee's reasonable belief that government misconduct has occurred. A careful review of the historical record indicates a generally faithful congressional adherence to these prudential considerations.

This report will briefly review the legal basis for investigative oversight, followed by several prominent examples of congressional oversight that reflect the significant breadth and reach of the legislative investigative prerogative vis-à-vis the Department. Next we will review and assess the Department's contentions, based on policy, common law, and constitutional privilege, that it has asserted to attempt to limit congressional access to agency information. An appendix to this report provides summaries of 20 inquiries in which committees have successfully obtained documents and testimony respecting a wide variety of Department materials and memoranda.

THE LEGAL BASIS FOR OVERSIGHT

Constitutional Authority to Perform Oversight and Investigative Inquiries

Generally, Congress's authority and power to obtain information, including, but not limited to, classified and/or confidential information, is extremely broad. While there is no express provision of the Constitution or specific statute authorizing the conduct of congressional oversight or investigations, the Supreme Court has firmly established that such power is essential to the legislative function as to be implied from the general vesting of legislative powers in Congress.[7] In *Eastland v. United States Serviceman's Fund*, for instance, the Court stated that the "scope of its power of inquiry ... is as penetrating and far-reaching as the potential power to enact and appropriate under the Constitution."[8] Also, in *Watkins v. United States*, the Court emphasized that the "power of the Congress to conduct investigations is inherent in the legislative process. That power is broad. It encompasses inquiries concerning the administration of existing laws as well as proposed or possibly needed statutes."[9] The Court further stressed that Congress's power to investigate is at its peak when focusing on alleged waste, fraud, abuse, or maladministration within a government department. Specifically, the Court explained that the investigative power "comprehends probes into departments of the federal government to expose corruption, inefficiency, or waste."[10] The Court went on to note that the first Congresses held "inquiries dealing with suspected corruption or mismanagement of government officials."[11] Given these factors, the Court recognized "the power of the Congress to inquire into and publicize corruption, maladministration, or inefficiencies in the agencies of Government."[12]

Legislative Purpose

While the congressional power of inquiry is broad, it is not unlimited. The Supreme Court has admonished that the power to investigate may be exercised only "in aid of the legislative function"[13] and cannot be used to expose for the sake of exposure alone. The *Watkins* Court underlined these limitations, stating that

> There is no general authority to expose the private affairs of individuals without justification in terms of the functions of the Congress ... nor is the Congress a law enforcement or trial agency. These are functions of the executive and judicial departments of government. No inquiry is an end in itself; it must be related to, and in furtherance of, a legitimate task of the Congress.[14]

A committee's inquiry must have a legislative purpose or be conducted pursuant to some other constitutional power of Congress, such as the authority of each House to discipline its own members, judge the returns of the their elections, and to conduct impeachment proceedings.[15] Although the 1927 Supreme Court decision in *Kilbourn v. Thompson*[16] held that the investigation in that case was an improper probe into the private affairs of individuals, the courts today generally will presume that there is a legislative purpose for an investigation. A House or Senate rule or resolution authorizing the investigation does not have to specifically state the committee's legislative purpose.[17] In *In re Chapman*,[18] the Court upheld the validity of a resolution authorizing an inquiry into charges of corruption against certain Senators despite the fact that it was silent as to what might be done when the investigation was completed. The Court stated the following:

> The questions were undoubtedly pertinent to the subject matter of the inquiry. The resolutions directed the committee to inquire "whether any Senator has been, or is, speculating in what are known as sugar stocks during the consideration of the tariff bill now before the Senate." What the Senate might or might not do upon the facts when ascertained, we cannot say nor are we called upon to inquire whether such ventures might be defensible, as contended in argument, but it is plain that negative answers would have cleared that body of what the Senate regarded as offensive imputations, while affirmative answers might have led to further action on the part of the Senate within its constitutional powers.
>
> Nor will it do to hold that the Senate had no jurisdiction to pursue the particular inquiry because the preamble and resolutions did not specify that the proceedings were taken for the purpose of censure or expulsion, if certain facts were disclosed by the investigation. The matter was within the range of the constitutional powers of the Senate. The resolutions adequately indicated that the transactions referred to were deemed by the Senate reprehensible and deserving of condemnation and punishment. The right to expel extends to all cases where the offense is such as in the judgment of the Senate is inconsistent with the trust and duty of a Member.
>
> We cannot assume on this record that the action of the Senate was without a legitimate object, and so encroach upon the province of that body. Indeed, we think it affirmatively appears that the Senate was acting within its right, and it was certainly not necessary that the resolutions should declare in advance what the Senate meditated doing when the investigation was concluded.[19]

In *McGrain v. Daugherty*,[20] the original resolution that authorized the Senate investigation into the Teapot Dome Affair[21] made no mention of a legislative purpose. A subsequent resolution for the attachment of a contumacious witness declared that his testimony was sought for the purpose of obtaining "information necessary as a basis for such legislative and other action as the Senate may deem necessary and proper."[22] The Court found that the investigation of the DOJ was ordered for a legitimate object. It wrote,

> The only legitimate object the Senate could have in ordering the investigation was to aid it in legislating, and we think the subject matter was such that the presumption should be indulged that this was the real object. An express avowal of the object would have been better; but in view of the particular subject-matter was not indispensable. ...
>
> The second resolution—the one directing the witness be attached—declares that this testimony is sought with the purpose of obtaining "information necessary as a basis for such legislative and other action as the Senate may deem necessary and proper." This avowal of contemplated legislation is in accord with what we think is the right interpretation of the earlier resolution directing the investigation. The suggested possibility of "other action" if deemed "necessary or proper" is of course open to criticism in that there is no other action in the matter which would be within the power of the Senate. But we do not assent to the view that this indefinite and untenable suggestion invalidates the entire proceeding. The right view in our opinion is that it takes nothing from the lawful object avowed in the same resolution and is rightly inferable from the earlier one. It is not as if an inadmissible or unlawful object were affirmatively and definitely avowed.[23]

The court also emphasized that the DOJ, like all other executive departments and agencies, is a creature of Congress and subject to its legislative and oversight authority.[24] Moreover, when the investigation's asserted purpose is supported by reference to specific problems which in the past have been, or in the future may be, the subject of appropriate legislation, it has been held that a court cannot say that a committee of Congress exceeds its power when it seeks information in such areas.[25] In the past, the types of legislative activity which have justified the exercise of the power to investigate have included the primary functions of legislating and appropriating,[26] the function of deciding whether or not legislation is appropriate,[27] oversight of the administration of the laws by the executive branch,[28] and the essential congressional function of informing itself in matters of national concern.[29] In addition, Congress's power to investigate such diverse matters as foreign and domestic subversive activities,[30] labor union corruption,[31] and organizations that violate the civil rights of others[32] have all been upheld by the Supreme Court.

Despite the Court's broad interpretation of legislative purpose, Congress's authority is not unlimited. Courts have held that a committee lacks a legislative purpose if it appears to be conducting a legislative trial rather than an investigation to assist in performing its legislative function.[33] Furthermore, although "there is no congressional power to expose for the sake of exposure,"[34] "so long as Congress acts in pursuance of its constitutional power, the Judiciary lacks authority to intervene on the basis of the motives which spurred the exercise of that power."[35]

THE DEPARTMENT'S HISTORICAL RESPONSES TO CONGRESSIONAL REQUESTS FOR INTERNAL DOJ DOCUMENTS AND COMMUNICATIONS

The executive branch has advanced several arguments for declining to provide information to Congress about open and closed civil and criminal proceedings, most famously articulated by then Attorney General Robert Jackson in 1941. These rationales have included a desire to avoid prejudicial pre-trial publicity, protecting the rights of innocent third parties, protecting the identity of confidential informants, preventing disclosure of the government's strategy in anticipated or pending judicial proceedings, avoiding a potential chilling effect on the exercise of prosecutorial discretion by DOJ attorneys, and precluding interference with the President's constitutional duty to faithfully execute the laws. In the 1941 opinion, Attorney General Jackson argued that "congressional or public access to [internal DOJ documents] would not be in the public interest" because it would "seriously prejudice law enforcement."[36]

Jackson's views were reiterated by Attorney General William French Smith in 1982 during the Superfund dispute,[37] there applying the policy to specific types of documents:

> [the documents withheld] are sensitive memoranda or notes by EPA attorneys and investigators reflecting enforcement strategy, legal analyses, lists of potential witnesses, settlement considerations and similar materials the disclosure of which might adversely affect a pending enforcement action, overall enforcement policy, or the rights of individuals.
>
> I continue to believe, as have my predecessors, that unrestricted dissemination of law enforcement files would prejudice the cause of

> effective law enforcement and, because the reasons for the policy of confidentiality are as sound and fundamental to the administration of justice today as they were forty years ago, I see no reason to depart from the consistent position of previous presidents and attorney generals.[38]

Acceding to congressional investigation demands, the Attorney General asserted, would make Congress "in a sense, a partner in the investigation... [raising] a substantial danger that congressional pressures will influence the course of the investigation."[39] This policy is said to be "premised in part on the fact that the Constitution vests in the President and his subordinates the responsibility to 'Take Care that the Laws be faithfully executed.'"[40]

In the 2001-2002 House Government Reform Committee investigation of the FBI misuse of informants,[41] the Department maintained its historic position of withholding internal deliberative prosecutorial documents, before finally disclosing the documents following increased congressional pressure. In a February 1, 2002, letter to Chairman Burton, the DOJ Assistant Attorney General for Legislative Affairs explained,

> Our particular concern in the current controversy pertains to the narrow and especially sensitive categories of advice memoranda to the Attorney General and the deliberative documents making recommendations regarding whether or not to bring criminal charges against individuals. We believe that the public interest in avoiding the polarization of the criminal justice process required greater protection of those documents which, in turn, influences the accommodation process. This is not an "inflexible position," but rather a statement of a principled interest in ensuring the integrity of prosecutorial decision-making.[42]

Finally, during the House Oversight investigation of Operation Fast and Furious, the DOJ resisted committee requests for access to internal deliberative communications made in response to the committee's investigation. The DOJ argued that their disclosure

> would inhibit the candor of such Executive Branch deliberations in the future and significantly impair the Executive Branch's ability to respond independently and effectively to congressional oversight. This would raise substantial separation of powers concerns and potentially create an imbalance in the relationship between these two co-equal branches of the government.[43]

ASSESSMENT OF THE DEPARTMENT'S OPPOSITION TO CONGRESSIONAL ACCESS TO INTERNAL DOJ MATERIALS

DOJ's Policy Objections to Disclosure: Concerns About Pre-Trial Publicity, Due Process, and Concurrent Investigations

As has been recounted previously, the Supreme Court has repeatedly reaffirmed the breadth of Congress' right to investigate the government's conduct of criminal and civil litigation.[44] The courts have also held that agencies may not deny Congress access to agency documents, even in situations where the inquiry may result in the exposure of criminal corruption or maladministration of agency officials. The Supreme Court has noted, "[B]ut surely a congressional committee which is engaged in a legitimate legislative investigation need not grind to a halt whenever responses to its inquiries might potentially be harmful to a witness in some distinct proceeding ... or when crime or wrongdoing is exposed."[45] The Court further explained:

> The suggestion made in dissent that the questions which petitioner refused to answer were 'outside the power of a committee to ask' under the Due Process Clause because they touched on matters then pending in judicial proceedings cannot be accepted for several reasons: First, the reasoning underlying this proposition is that these inquiries constituted a legislative encroachment on the judicial function. But such reasoning can hardly be limited to inquiries that may be germane to existing judicial proceedings: it would surely apply as well to inquiries calling for answers that may be used to the prejudice of witnesses in any future judicial proceeding. If such were the reach of 'due process' it would turn a witness' privilege against self-incrimination into a self-operating restraint on congressional inquiry, and would in effect pro tanto obliterate the need for that constitutional protection.[46]

Additionally, the pendency of litigation does not prohibit Congress from investigating facts that have a bearing on that litigation, where the information sought is needed to determine what, if any, legislation should be enacted to prevent further ills.[47]

Although several lower court decisions have recognized that congressional hearings may generate prejudicial pre-trial publicity, they have not expressly suggested that there are any constitutional or legal limitations on Congress's right to conduct an investigation while judicial proceedings are pending. Instead, the cases have suggested approaches, such as granting a continuance or a change of venue, to deal with the publicity problem.[48] For example, the court in one of the leading cases, *Delaney v. United States,* stated that "no doubt that the committee acted lawfully, within the constitutional powers of Congress duly delegated to it" but went on to describe the possible consequences of concurrent executive and congressional investigations:

> We think that the United States is put to a choice in this matter: If the United States, through its legislative department, acting conscientiously pursuant to its conception of the public interest, chooses to hold a public hearing inevitably resulting in such damaging publicity prejudicial to a person awaiting trial on a pending indictment, then the United States must accept the consequences that the judicial department, charged with the duty of assuring the defendant a fair trial before an impartial jury, may find it necessary to postpone the trial until by lapse of time the danger of the prejudice may reasonably be thought to have been substantially removed.[49]

The *Delaney* court distinguished the case of a congressional hearing generating publicity relating to an individual not under indictment at the time:

> Such a situation may present important differences from the instant case. In such a situation the investigative function of Congress has its greatest utility: Congress is informing itself so that it may take appropriate legislative action; it is informing the Executive so that existing laws may be enforced; and it is informing the public so that democratic processes may be brought to bear to correct any disclosed executive laxity. Also, if as a result of such legislative hearing an indictment is eventually procured against the public official, then in the normal case there would be a much greater lapse of time between the publicity accompanying the public hearing and the trial of the subsequently indicted official than would be the case if the legislative hearing were held while the accused is awaiting trial on a pending indictment.[50]

The absence of an indictment and the length of time between a congressional hearing and criminal trial have been factors considered by courts that reject claims that congressionally generated publicity prejudiced defendants.[51] Finally, in the context of adjudicatory administrative proceedings, courts on occasion have held that pressures caused by Members of Congress questioning agency decision makers may be sufficient to undermine the impartiality of the proceeding.[52] But the courts have also made clear that mere inquiry and oversight of agency actions, including agency proceedings that are quasi-adjudicatory in nature, will not be held to rise to the level of political pressure, designed to influence particular proceedings, that would require judicial condemnation.[53]

Thus, the courts have recognized the potentially prejudicial effect congressional hearings can have on pending cases. While not directly questioning its prerogatives with respect to oversight and investigation, the cases pose a choice for the Congress. It faces weighing the harm caused by congressionally generated publicity to the prosecutorial effort of the executive against the fact that access to information under secure conditions can fulfill the congressional power of investigation. The observation of the Iran-Contra Independent Counsel is pertinent here: "The legislative branch has the power to decide whether it is more important perhaps to destroy a prosecution than to hold back testimony they need. They make that decision. It is not a judicial decision, or a legal decision, but a political decision of the highest importance."[54]

Assertion of Common Law and Constitutional Privileges Against Disclosure

In the past the executive frequently has made a broad claim that prosecution is an inherently executive function and that congressional access to information related to the exercise of that function is thereby limited. Citing the "need to protect the government's ability to prosecute fully and fairly," the executive views questions about the exercise of prosecutorial discretion and demands for access to open law enforcement files as beyond the scope of proper congressional inquiry. The executive views these inquiries as interfering with the discretion traditionally enjoyed by the prosecutor with respect to pursuing criminal cases.[55] Similarly, the Justice Department has objected to releasing internal deliberative documents, since it believes their disclosure would substantially chill future deliberations.[56] These concerns are usually resolved through the traditional negotiation and accommodation process.[57] However, in rare instances the executive branch may respond to a congressional demand to produce information with an assertion of executive privilege by the President. For example, during the congressional investigation of Operation Fast and Furious, the DOJ released numerous documents related to the program, but President Obama specifically claimed executive privilege over DOJ internal documents that were responsive to the committee's subpoena.[58]

In the few controversies that have reached a judicial forum, federal courts have been highly reluctant to rule on the merits.[59] For example, in *United States v. AT&T*,[60] the Justice Department sought to enjoin a congressional subpoena for letters the FBI sent to AT&T. The D.C. District Court held that there is a constitutional duty for the executive and Congress to attempt to accommodate each other's needs, and refused to resolve the dispute because both branches had not yet done so. The court displayed the same reluctance in *United States v. House of Representatives*,[61] where it dismissed a Justice Department suit seeking a declaratory judgment that the Administrator of the Environmental Protection Agency (EPA), Anne Gorsuch Burford, "acted lawfully in refusing to release certain documents to a congressional subcommittee" at the direction of the President.[62] The court dismissed the case, without reaching the executive privilege claim, on the ground that judicial intervention in a dispute "concerning the respective powers of the Legislative and Executive Branches ... should be delayed until all possibilities for settlement have been exhausted. ... Compromise and cooperation, rather than confrontation, should be the aim of the parties."[63] Finally, the D.C. Circuit Court sketched the outer limits of the executive's power to withhold information in *Committee on the Judiciary v. Miers*,[64] unequivocally rejecting the executive's claim that present and past senior advisers to the President—in this case former White House Counsel Harriet Miers and Chief of Staff Joshua Bolten—were absolutely immune from compelled congressional process. However, the case did not provide any discussion of the merits of the specific claims of executive privilege, but rather held that executive privilege could be asserted "in response to any specific questions posed by the Committee" while providing testimony.[65]

If a court does reach the merits of an executive privilege claim asserted against a congressional inquiry, its analysis may be influenced by *In re Sealed Case (Espy)*[66] and *Judicial Watch v. Department of Justice*,[67] two D.C. Circuit cases that addressed issues left unresolved by the Watergate executive privilege cases.[68] The *Espy* case distinguished between the "presidential communications privilege" and the "deliberative process privilege." Both, the court observed, are executive privileges designed to protect the confidentiality of executive branch decision making. The deliberative process privilege, which applies to executive branch officials generally, is a common law privilege that requires a lower threshold of need to be overcome, and "disappears altogether when there is any reason to believe government misconduct has occurred."[69] On the other hand, the court explained, the presidential communications privilege is rooted in "constitutional separation of powers principles and the President's unique constitutional role" and applies only to "direct decisionmaking by the President."[70] The privilege may be overcome only by a substantial showing that "the subpoenaed materials likely contain[] important evidence" and that "the evidence is not available with due diligence elsewhere."[71] The court held that the presidential communications privilege covers communications authored or solicited and received by close presidential advisers in the course of preparing advice for the President even if those communications are not made directly to the President. The court, however, carefully restricted its reach by explicitly confining the privilege to staff within the executive office of the President that has "operational proximity" to the President.

The D.C. Circuit affirmed the limits of the privilege in *Judicial Watch*, a case involving requests for documents about pardon applications reviewed by the Justice Department's Office of the Pardon Attorney and the Deputy Attorney General for consideration by President Clinton.[72] The district court held that because the materials sought had been produced for the sole purpose of advising the President on a "quintessential and non-delegable Presidential power"—the exercise of the President's constitutional pardon authority—the presidential communications privilege applied.[73] The appeals court reversed, explaining that the privilege may be invoked only when documents or communications are authored or solicited and received by the President himself or by presidential advisers in close proximity to the President who have significant responsibility for advising him on matters requiring presidential decision making.[74] While the exercise of the President's pardon power was certainly a non-delegable, core presidential function, the officials involved, the Deputy Attorney General and the Pardon Attorney, were deemed to be too removed from the President and his senior White House advisers to be protected by the privilege.[75]

These two D.C. Circuit cases appear to highlight two key considerations that should be examined when determining if the presidential communications privilege can be properly asserted. First, the protected communication must be "authored or solicited and received by"[76] the President or a close White House advisor with "operational proximity" to the President.[77] Second, a communication may have to relate to decision making in the context of a "quintessential and non-delegable presidential power." *Espy* and *Judicial*

Watch do not establish this as a requirement for applying the presidential communications privilege. However, both cases deal exclusively with quintessential and non-delegable presidential powers—the appointment and removal and pardon power. Therefore, one could argue that the Presidential communications privilege is limited to exclude materials concerning presidential decision making pursuant to statutory delegations of authority to the President or other executive branch officials.

If an executive privilege claim was challenged in litigation that proceeded to the merits of the claim, the DOJ may argue that the materials withheld are properly covered under the presidential communications privilege. If the materials satisfied the "operational proximity" test laid out above, the DOJ would then have to confront the type of decision making being exercised in the materials. In the case of a claim based on prosecutorial discretion, the Supreme Court's ruling in *Morrison v. Olson*[78]—sustaining the validity of the appointment and removal conditions for independent counsels under the Ethics in Government Act—casts doubt on whether prosecution is a quintessential and non-delegable presidential power. The Court held that the exercise of prosecutorial discretion is in no way "central" to the functioning of the executive branch[79] and rejected a claim that insulating the independent counsel from at-will presidential removal interfered with the President's duty to "take care" that the laws be faithfully executed. If a court determined that the presidential communications privilege could only apply to decision making related to quintessential and non-delegable presidential powers, the reasoning in *Morrison* may prevent the DOJ from successfully shielding Congress from accessing materials regarding prosecutorial discretion by asserting this privilege.

Even if certain documents fall within the presidential communications privilege, this does not necessarily mean that disclosure of the documents can never be compelled by Congress. The Supreme Court in *U.S. v. Nixon* made clear, in the context of a subpoena for information from a special prosecutor for use in a criminal proceeding, that executive privilege is not absolute, but rather remains a qualified privilege. While the Supreme Court has not addressed executive privilege in the face of a congressional demand for information, the D.C. Circuit has stated that the presidential communications privilege may be overcome where the "subpoenaed evidence is demonstrably critical to the responsible fulfillment of the Committee's functions."[80]

If a court finds that the withheld material does not qualify under the presidential communication privilege, then the executive may fall back on the less comprehensive deliberative process privilege. A "deliberative process" claim may be viewed as a common law privilege available to executive agencies that may be overcome by a showing of need by an investigatory body and, as *Espy* noted, "disappears" when that body reasonably believes that government misconduct has occurred.[81] No court has delineated the precise weight afforded to common law privileges in the face of a congressional investigation. In practice, the committee exercises its own discretion in deciding whether to accept the assertion of common law privileges. For example, when faced with a claim of attorney-client privilege, a common law privilege, a committee has "weigh[ed] the legislative need for disclosure against any possible resulting injury."[82] The legal basis for Congress's practice in this area is based upon its implicit constitutional prerogative to investigate, which has been long recognized by the Supreme Court as broad, and at its peak when the subject is waste, fraud, abuse, or maladministration within a government department.[83] Common law privileges are not constitutionally based, but rather judge-made exceptions to the normal principle of full disclosure in the adversary process.[84] Thus, a demonstration of need by a jurisdictional committee in most circumstances would appear to be sufficient to overcome common law privileges. An opinion issued by the Legal Ethics Committee of the District of Columbia Bar in 1999 clearly acknowledges the long-standing congressional practice of exercising discretion over acceptance of common law privileges like attorney-client privilege.[85] The D.C. Bar opinion urges attorneys to press every appropriate objection to a congressional subpoena that demands disclosure of information subject to the attorney-client privilege until no further avenues of appeal are available.[86] However, it also allows the attorney to disclose the materials subject to attorney-client privilege at the earliest point that he is put in legal jeopardy, such as being threatened with a contempt of Congress action.

APPENDIX. SELECTED CONGRESSIONAL INVESTIGATIONS OF THE DEPARTMENT OF JUSTICE, 1920-2012

This *Appendix* consists of brief summaries of 21 significant congressional investigations of the Department of Justice that involved either open or closed investigations. In each case, the Department agreed to supply documents pertaining to those investigations, including prosecutorial decision-making memoranda and correspondence, or to make high ranking officials and subordinate employees, such as line attorneys and investigative personnel, available for staff interviews and testimony before committees. These investigations demonstrate that DOJ has consistently been subjected to congressional oversight, which has examined misconduct in the Justice Department and elsewhere. A number of these investigations spawned seminal Supreme Court rulings that today provide the foundation for the generally broad congressional power of inquiry discussed above. In most cases, the DOJ claimed that committee demands for documents and testimony were precluded either by a constitutional or common law privilege or executive branch policy. In many cases, investigating congressional committees were provided with documents regarding closed cases that were considered to be "sensitive" materials.[87] Several of these inquiries appear to have led to important remedial legislation and the resignations[88] and convictions[89] of several Attorneys General. While this appendix examines many notable instances of congressional investigations of the DOJ, it is not an exhaustive list of such inquiries.

Palmer Raids

In 1920 and 1921, investigations were held in the Senate and House into the so-called "Palmer raids" in which, under the direction of Attorney General A. Mitchell Palmer, thousands of suspected Communists and others allegedly advocating the overthrow of the government were arrested and deported.[90] Attorney General Palmer, accompanied by his Special Assistant, J. Edgar Hoover, during three days of testimony at Senate hearings discussed the details of numerous deportation cases, including cases that were on appeal.[91] In support of his testimony, Palmer provided the Subcommittee with various Department memoranda and correspondence, including Bureau of Investigation reports concerning the deportation cases.[92] Among the materials provided were the Department's confidential instructions to the Bureau outlining the procedures to be followed in the surveillance and arrest of the suspected Communists,[93] and a lengthy "memorandum of comments and analysis" prepared by one of Palmer's special assistants, which responded to a district court opinion, pending appeal, that was critical of the Department's actions in these deportation cases.[94]

Teapot Dome

Several years later, the Senate conducted an investigation of the Teapot Dome scandal. While the Senate Committee on Public Lands and Surveys focused on the actions of the Department of the Interior in leasing naval oil reserves, a Senate Select Committee was constituted to investigate "charges of misfeasance and nonfeasance in the Department of Justice,"[95] in failing to prosecute wrongdoers in the Department of the Interior, as well as other cases.[96] The Select Committee heard from scores of present and former attorneys and agents of the Department and its Bureau of Investigation, who offered detailed testimony about specific instances of the Department's failure to prosecute alleged meritorious cases. Not all of the cases upon which testimony was offered were closed, as one of the Committee's goals in its questioning was to identify cases where the statute of limitations had not run out and prosecution was still possible.[97]

The committee also obtained access to DOJ documentation, including prosecutorial memoranda, on a wide range of matters. However, given the charges of widespread corruption in the Department and the imminent resignation of Attorney General Daugherty, it would appear that some of the documents furnished to the Committee early in the hearings may have been volunteered by the witnesses and not officially provided by the Department. Although Attorney General Daugherty had promised cooperation with the committee, and had agreed to provide access to at least the files of closed cases,[98] such cooperation apparently had not been forthcoming.[99]

In two instances immediately following Daugherty's resignation, the Committee was refused access to confidential Bureau of Investigation investigative reports pending the appointment of a new Attorney General who could advise the President about such production.[100] Witnesses from the Department were still permitted to testify about the investigations that were the subject of the reports and were even allowed to read from the reports at the hearings. With the appointment of the new Attorney General, Harlan F. Stone, the Committee was granted broad access to Department files. Committee Chairman Smith Brookhard remarked that "[Stone] is furnishing us with all the files we want, whereas the former Attorney General, Mr. Daugherty, refused nearly all that we asked."[101] For example, with the authorization of the new Attorney General, an accountant with the Department who had led an investigation of fraudulent sales of property by the Alien Property Custodian's office appeared and produced his confidential reports written to the Bureau of Investigation. The reports described the factual findings from his investigation and his recommendations for further action, and included the names of companies and individuals suspected of making false claims. The Department had not acted on those recommendations, though the cases had not been closed.[102] A similar investigative report, concerning an inquiry into the disappearance of large quantities of liquor under the control of the Department during Harding Administration, was also produced.[103]

As part of its investigation, the Select Committee issued a subpoena for the testimony of Mally S. Daugherty, the brother of the Attorney General. After Mally Daugherty failed to respond to the subpoena, the Senate sent its Deputy Sergeant at Arms to take him into custody and bring him before the Senate. Following his detention by the Deputy Sergeant at Arms, Daugherty petitioned in federal court for a writ of habeas corpus arguing that the Senate's investigation had exceeded its constitutional powers. The case ultimately reached the Supreme Court, where, in a landmark decision,[104] the Court upheld the Senate's authority to investigate these charges concerning the Department:

> [T]he subject to be investigated was the administration of the Department of Justice— whether its functions were being properly discharged or were being neglected or misdirected, and particularly whether the Attorney General and his assistants were performing or neglecting their duties in respect of the institution and prosecution of proceedings to punish crimes and enforce appropriate remedies against the wrongdoers—specific instances of alleged neglect being recited. Plainly the subject was one on which legislation could be had and would be materially aided by the information which the investigation was calculated to elicit.[105]

In another Teapot Dome case that reached the Supreme Court, *Sinclair v. United States*,[106] a different witness at the congressional hearings refused to answer questions, and was prosecuted for contempt of Congress. The witness had noted that a lawsuit had been commenced between the government and the Mammoth Oil Company, and declared, "I shall reserve any evidence I may be able to give for those courts ... and shall respectfully decline to answer any questions propounded by your committee."[107] The Supreme Court upheld the witness' conviction for contempt of Congress. The Court considered and rejected in unequivocal terms the witness's contention that the pendency of lawsuits provided an excuse for withholding information. Neither the laws directing that such lawsuits be instituted, nor the lawsuits themselves, "operated to divest the Senate, or the committee, of power further to investigate the actual administration of the land laws."[108] The Court further explained:

> It may be conceded that Congress is without authority to compel disclosure for the purpose of aiding the prosecution of pending suits; but the authority of that body, directly or through its committees to require pertinent disclosures in aid of its own constitutional power is not abridged because the information sought to be elicited may also be of use in such suits.[109]

Investigations of the DOJ During the 1950's

In 1952, the Special Subcommittee to Investigate the Department of Justice of the House Committee on the Judiciary was constituted. The subcommittee conducted a lengthy investigation from 1952 to 1953, developing thousands of pages of testimony on a range of allegations of abuses and inefficiencies in the Department.[110] Among the subjects of inquiry considered during these hearings were the following.

1. Grand Jury Curbing

Extensive testimony was heard about a charge that the Department had attempted improperly to curb a St. Louis grand jury inquiry into the failure to enforce federal tax fraud laws. After taking testimony in executive session from one witness, the subcommittee suspended its hearings on this subject pending the discharge of the grand jury.[111] The subcommittee resumed its hearings several months later, at which time testimony was taken from the former Attorney General, a former Assistant Attorney General, the Chief of the appellate section of the Tax Division, and an Assistant U.S. Attorney. Several members of the St. Louis grand jury also testified before the subcommittee. In addition to intradepartmental correspondence,[112] among the materials that the subcommittee reviewed and included in the public record were transcripts of telephone conversations between various DOJ attorneys concerning the grand jury investigation.[113]

The subcommittee began its hearings on the handling of the St. Louis grand jury with a statement emphasizing that its interest "is merely to ascertain whether or not there was in fact any attempt by the Department of Justice to influence the grand jury in its investigation,"[114] and that "the members of the subcommittee and counsel are aware of the rule of strict secrecy surrounding the proceedings of any grand jury. Mindful of that, our questioning will not touch upon any specific case or evidence that may have been presented to the grand jury."[115] The subcommittee's questions to the grand jurors focused on efforts by Department attorneys to prevent them from conducting a thorough investigation and on whether the grand jury had been pressured by those attorneys to issue a report absolving the government of impropriety in its handling of tax fraud cases.[116] The present and former Department attorneys who testified were asked similar questions,[117] and at one point the subcommittee asked for, and an Assistant U.S. Attorney provided, the names of certain witnesses who had appeared before the grand jury.[118] Later that same year, the subcommittee examined similar charges of DOJ interference with another grand jury, which had been investigating Communist infiltration of the United Nations. The subcommittee received testimony from a number of grand jurors and Department attorneys, including then Criminal Division attorney Roy Cohn.[119] The subcommittee's chief counsel again cautioned that "[t]he sanctity of the grand jury as a process of American justice must be protected at all costs," and stated that the subcommittee was seeking information solely relating to attempts to delay or otherwise influence the grand jurors' deliberations, not information that would reveal the actual testimony of witnesses appearing before them.[120]

2. Prosecution of Routine Cases

Attorney General McGrath resigned in April 1952, in part in response to the evidence uncovered by the subcommittee of corruption in the Department, particularly in the Tax Division. After the replacement of McGrath by James P. McGranery, and the Administration's concern about these corruption reports, the subcommittee observed "a new and refreshing attitude of cooperation which soon appeared at all levels in the Department of Justice."[121] The subcommittee declared that "its work has been limited only by the capacity of its staff to digest the sheer volume of available fact and documentary evidence relating to the Department's work. Everything that has been requested has been furnished, including file materials and administrative memoranda which had previously been withheld."[122]

For example, in investigating charges that the Department was often dilatory in its handling of routine cases, the subcommittee staff undertook a detailed analysis of a number of cases in which delay was alleged to have occurred. To demonstrate publicly the nature of this problem, the subcommittee chose a procurement fraud case that had been recently closed, and conducted a "public file review" of the case at a subcommittee hearing.

Attorneys from the Department at the hearing went document by document through the Department's file in the case.[123] The subcommittee was granted access to all of the documentation collected in the case, with the exception of confidential FBI reports that the subcommittee had agreed not to seek. However, certain communications from the FBI to the Department concerning the prosecution of the case were provided.[124]

3. New York City Police Brutality

During the 83rd Congress, the subcommittee turned to allegations that the Criminal Division had entered into an agreement with the New York City Police Department (NYPD) not to prosecute instances of police brutality by New York police officers that might be violations of federal civil rights statutes. The subcommittee stated that its purpose was not to inquire into the merits of particular cases, only to ascertain whether DOJ and the NYPD had entered into such an agreement.[125] Justice Department witnesses had also been instructed by the Attorney General not to discuss the merits of any pending cases.[126]

Department witnesses included a former Attorney General, several present and former Assistant Attorneys General, as well as other Department attorneys and FBI agents.[127] The substance of earlier meetings between Department officials and the New York City Police Commissioner in which this arrangement was allegedly agreed to was probed in depth. Although questions concerning the merits of specific cases were avoided, the subcommittee obtained from these witnesses a chronology of the Department's actions in a number of cases. The subcommittee received DOJ memoranda and correspondence, as well as telephone transcripts of the intradepartmental conversations of a U.S. Attorney.[128]

Investigation of Consent Decree Program

In 1957 and 1958, the Antitrust Subcommittee of the House Judiciary Committee conducted an inquiry into the negotiation, enforcement, and competitive effect of consent decrees by the DOJ Antitrust Division, with particular emphasis on consent decrees that had been recently entered into with the oil-pipeline industry and AT&T.[129] The subcommittee developed a 4,492-page hearing record, holding seventeen days of hearings on the AT&T consent decree and four days of hearings on the oil pipeline consent decree.

The subcommittee experienced what it viewed as a lack of cooperation from the Department throughout its investigation, stating that "[t]he extent to which the Department of Justice went to withhold information from the committee in this investigation is unparalleled in the committee's experience."[130] The subcommittee's chairman, requesting that the Attorney General disclose "all files in the Department of Justice relating to the negotiations for, and signing of, a consent decree" with AT&T.[131] The DOJ unconditionally refused to grant the subcommittee access to any of these documents. Deputy Attorney General William P. Rogers asserted two grounds to support the Department's refusal to cooperate. First, Rogers maintained that since the files contained information voluntarily submitted by AT&T in the course of consent decree negotiations, disclosing the files to the subcommittee "would violate the confidential nature of settlement negotiations and, in the process, discourage defendants, present and future, from entering into such negotiations."[132] In a later letter, the head of the Antitrust Division, Victor Hansen, added that "[t]hose considerations which require that the Department treat on a confidential basis communications with a defendant during consent decree negotiations also apply to the enforcement of a decree."[133]

Second, Rogers argued that the "essential process of full and flexible exchange" of ideas when crafting memoranda and recommendations would be "seriously endangered were staff members hampered by the knowledge they might at some later date be forced to explain before Congress intermediate positions taken."[134] Rogers stated that the DOJ's refusal to comply was in accordance with an earlier directive from the President to the Department to that effect, which provided:

> Because it is essential to efficient and effective administration that employees of the executive branch be in a position to be completely candid in advising with each other on official matters, and because it is not in the public interest that any of their conversations or communications, or any documents or reproductions, concerning such advice be disclosed, you will instruct employees of your Department that in all of their appearances before [congressional] committees not to testify to any such conversations or communications or to produce any such document or reproductions. This principle must be maintained regardless of who would be benefitted by such disclosures.[135]

The subcommittee asserted in its final report that initially the "Attorney General refused access to the files of the Department of Justice primarily in order to prevent disclosure of facts that might prove embarrassing to the Department."[136] The subcommittee further concluded that such withholding had "materially hampered the committee's investigation."[137] However, it may be noted that the subcommittee was ultimately able to obtain much of the material concerning the AT&T consent decree that DOJ refused to provide directly from AT&T itself.[138]

The Department was, however, somewhat more forthcoming in permitting attorneys to testify about the AT&T consent decree. For example, the head of the Antitrust Division informed two Division attorneys, who had dissented from the decision to enter into the AT&T consent decree and were called to testify, that "we do not at the present time think it appropriate ... to ... assert any privilege on behalf of the Department with regard to any information within [your] knowledge which is relevant to the negotiations of the decree in the Western Electric case."[139] These two attorneys later testified before the subcommittee about those negotiations, including their reasons for differing with the Department's decision to enter into the consent decree.[140]

Cointelpro and Related Investigations of FBI-DOJ Misconduct

Between 1974 and 1978, Senate and House committees examined the intelligence operations of a number of federal agencies, including the domestic intelligence operations of the FBI and various units of the Justice Department, such as the Interdivision Information Unit.[141] A Senate Select Committee examined 800 witnesses: 50 in public session, 250 in executive sessions, and the balance in interviews.[142] A number of those providing public testimony were present and former FBI and DOJ officials.

The Select Committee estimated it had obtained approximately 110,000 pages of documents from these intelligence agencies and other sources, with still more being preliminarily reviewed at the agencies.[143] Hundreds of FBI documents were reprinted as hearing exhibits, though "[u]nder criteria determined by the Committee, in consultation with the Federal Bureau of Investigation, certain materials were deleted from these exhibits to maintain the integrity of the internal operating procedures of the FBI. Further deletions were made with respect to protecting the privacy of certain individuals and groups. These deletions do not change the material content of these exhibits."[144] The Select Committee concluded in its final report that the "most important lesson" learned from its investigation was that "effective oversight is impossible without regular access to the underlying working documents of the intelligence community. Top level briefings do not adequately describe the realities. For that the documents are a necessary supplement and at times the only source."[145]

Hearings on FBI domestic intelligence operations also were held before the House Judiciary Subcommittee on Civil and Constitutional Rights beginning in 1975. A number of DOJ and FBI officials testified, including Attorneys General Edward Levi and Griffin Bell and FBI Director Clarence Kelly. At the request of the chairman of the Judiciary Committee, the General Accounting Office (GAO) also began a review of FBI operations in this area in 1974.[146] In an attempt to analyze current FBI practices, the GAO chose ten FBI offices involved in varying levels of domestic intelligence activity, and randomly selected 899 cases from those offices that year to review.[147]

The FBI agreed to GAO's proposal to have FBI agents prepare a summary of each selected cases' file. These summaries described the information that led to opening the investigation, the methods and sources used to collect information for the case, instructions from FBI Headquarters, and a brief summary of each document in the file. After reviewing the summaries, GAO staff held interviews with the FBI agents involved with the cases, as well as the agents who prepared the summaries.[148]

These hearings were continued in 1977 to hear the results of a similar GAO review of the FBI's domestic intelligence operations under new domestic security guidelines established by the Attorney General in 1976. In its follow-up investigation, GAO reviewed 319 additional randomly selected cases. As in its earlier review, GAO obtained FBI case summaries and then conducted agent interviews. This time, however, the Department also granted GAO access to copies of selected documents for verification purposes, with the names of informers and other sensitive data excised.[149]

White Collar Crime in the Oil Industry

In 1979, joint hearings were held by the Subcommittee on Energy and Power of the House Committee on Interstate and Foreign Commerce and the Subcommittee on Crime of the House Judiciary Committee to conduct an inquiry into allegations of fraudulent pricing of fuel in the oil industry and the failure of the Department of Energy and DOJ to effectively investigate and prosecute alleged criminality.[150] During the course of the hearings, testimony and evidence were received in closed session regarding open cases in which indictments were pending and criminal proceedings were in progress. The chairman of the Subcommittee on Energy and Power remarked:

> We know indictments are outstanding. We do not wish to interfere with rights of any parties to a fair trial. To this end we have scrupulously avoided any actions that might have affected the indictment of any party. In these hearings we will restrict our questions to the process and the general schemes to defraud and the failure of the Government to pursue these cases. Evidence and comments on specific cases must be left to the prosecutors in the cases they bring to trial.[151]

DOJ's Deputy Attorney General, Criminal Division, praised the Chairmen and committee members for their discreet conduct of the hearings: "I would like to commend Chairman Conyers, Chairman Dingell, and all other members of the committee and staff for the sensitivity which they have shown during the course of these hearings to the fact that we have ongoing criminal investigations and proceedings, and the appropriate handling of the question in order not to interfere with those investigations and criminal trials."[152]

The committees requested access to declination memoranda and the Justice Department stated that it had no objection, except to request that the information not be made public unless the committees had a compelling need. During the course of the hearing a DOJ staff attorney testified in open session as to the reason for not going forward with a particular criminal prosecution.

Although a civil prosecution of the same matter was then pending, DOJ agreed to supply the committees with documents leading to the decision not to prosecute.[153]

Billy Carter/Libya Investigation

A special subcommittee of the Senate Committee on the Judiciary was constituted in 1980 to investigate the activities of individuals representing the interests of foreign governments. Due to the short time frame that was given to report its conclusions to the Senate, the subcommittee narrowed the focus of its inquiry to the activities of the President's brother, Billy Carter, on behalf of the Libyan government.[154] A significant portion of this inquiry concerned the Department's handling of its investigation of Billy Carter, in particular whether Attorney General Benjamin R. Civiletti acted improperly by withholding certain intelligence information about Billy Carter's contacts with Libya from the Criminal Division attorneys responsible for the investigation, or had otherwise sought to influence the disposition of the case.

Although there was early disagreement as to the extent of the subcommittee's access to certain White House information, DOJ made no attempt to limit the subcommittee's access to the attorneys involved with the Billy Carter case. The subcommittee heard testimony from several representatives of the Department, including Attorney General Civiletti, and the Assistant Attorney General in charge of the Criminal Division, and three of his assistants. These witnesses testified about various topics, including the general structure of decision making in the Department, the nature of the Billy Carter investigation, the Attorney General's failure to communicate intelligence information concerning Billy Carter to the Criminal Division attorneys immediately, the decision to proceed civilly and not criminally against Carter, and the effect of various actions of the Attorney General and the White House on that prosecutorial decision.[155] The subcommittee also took depositions from some of these witnesses. Pursuant to a Senate Resolution providing it with such power, subcommittee staff took 35 depositions, totaling 2,646 pages.[156]

The subcommittee also was given access to documents from the Department's files on the Billy Carter case. The materials obtained included prosecutorial memoranda, correspondence between the Department and Billy Carter, the handwritten notes of the attorney in charge of the Foreign Agents Registration Unit of the Criminal Division, and FBI investigative reports and summaries of interviews with Billy Carter and his associates.[157] Not included in the public record were a number of classified documents, which were forwarded to and kept in the files of the Senate Intelligence Committee. These classified documents were available for examination by designated staff members and the Intelligence Committee, and some of the subcommittee documents were later used by the subcommittee in executive session.

Undercover Law Enforcement Activities (ABSCAM)

In 1982, the Senate established a select committee to study the undercover law enforcement activities of the FBI and other components of the Department of Justice.[158] Representatives from the Department, including FBI Director William Webster, testified generally about the history of the DOJ's undercover operations, their benefits and costs, and the policies governing the institution and supervision of such operations, including several sets of guidelines promulgated by the Attorney General. These witnesses also testified about

Abscam and several other specific undercover operations conducted by the FBI and other units of the Department.[159]

In addition to the public testimony from Department witnesses, committee staff conducted interviews with a number of present and former Department attorneys and FBI agents.[160] Among those testifying or interviewed were several present and former members of the Department's Brooklyn Organized Crime Strike Force. The Department told the committee that it "does not normally permit Strike Force attorneys to testify before congressional committees [and has] traditionally resisted questioning of this kind because it tends to inhibit prosecutors from proceeding through their normal tasks free from the fear that they may be second-guessed, with the benefit of hindsight, long after they take actions and make difficult judgements in the course of their duties."[161] The Department, nevertheless, agreed to this testimony, "because of their value to you as fact witnesses and because you have assured us that they will be asked to testify solely as to matters of fact within their personal knowledge and not conclusions or matters of policy."[162]

The most extensive focus of the committee's inquiry was on the FBI's Abscam operation, which lasted from early 1978 through January 1980, and resulted in the criminal conviction of one Senator, six Members of the House of Representatives, several local officials, and others. As part of this review, the subcommittee was "given access to almost all of the confidential documents generated during the covert stage of the undercover operation known as Abscam."[163] In all, the committee reviewed more than 20,000 pages of Abscam documents, as well as video and audio tapes and tape transcripts,[164] provided under the terms of an elaborate access agreement negotiated with the Department.

Pursuant to the agreement, the subcommittee was provided copies of confidential Abscam materials other than grand jury materials barred from disclosure under the Federal Rules of Criminal Procedure[165] and certain prosecutorial memoranda from the Abscam cases. Under the agreement, the Department was also permitted to withhold from the committee documents that might compromise ongoing investigations or reveal sensitive sources or investigative techniques.

However, the Department was required to describe each such document withheld, explain the basis of the denial, and give the committee an opportunity to propose conditions under which the documents might be provided. The committee further agreed to a "pledge of confidentiality" under which it was permitted to use and publicly disclose information derived from the confidential documents and to state that the information came from Department files, but was prohibited from publicly identifying the specific documents from which the information was obtained. All confidential documents were kept in a secure room, with access limited to the committee's members, its two counsel, and several designated document custodians.[166] Later, DOJ agreed to permit access to those materials by other committee attorneys as well.

In addition to the documents to which it was given direct access, the committee received extensive oral briefings, including direct quotations, on basic factual material from the withheld prosecutorial memoranda and documents prepared or compiled by the Department's Office of Professional Responsibility as part of an internal investigation of possible misconduct in the Abscam operations and prosecutions.[167]

Under the general framework established by this agreement, there was considerable give and take between the committee and the Department as to the degree of access that would be provided to specific documents. For example, the committee's counsel had sought access to a report prepared in the Criminal Division on FBI undercover operations.[168] The committee's chairman had also written to the Attorney General requesting access to that report.[169] An agreement was reached whereby the report could be examined by committee members or counsel at the Department and notes taken on its contents, but it could neither be copied nor removed from the Department.[170] Committee counsel utilized this procedure, but the committee determined that such limited access made it impractical for its members to personally review the report, and the committee's chairman again wrote the Attorney General asking him to release a copy.[171] The Department ultimately agreed to provide a copy of the report to each member of the committee, with the understanding that the report would not be disseminated beyond the members of the committee and its counsel, no additional copies would be made, and the copies provided by the Department would be returned at the conclusion of the committee's work.[172] Finally, the committee retained the right under the access agreement to seek unrestricted access to documents if it determined that the limited access set forth in the agreement was insufficient to permit it to effectively conduct its investigation.[173]

A similar investigation was conducted by the House Judiciary Subcommittee on Civil and Constitutional Rights, which held a total of 21 hearings over a period of four years.[174] The subcommittee examined in detail the FBI's Operation Corkscrew undercover operation, an investigation of alleged corruption in the Cleveland Municipal Court, with access to confidential Department documents provided to it under an agreement patterned after the access agreement negotiated by the Senate select committee investigating Abscam.[175]

Investigation of Withholding of EPA Documents

Burford I: The Superfund Investigation

In 1982, during the second session of the 97th Congress, the House Transportation Committee's Public Works Subcommittee on Oversight and the House Energy and Commerce's Subcommittee on Oversight and Investigations initiated investigations of the Environmental Protection Agency's (EPA) enforcement of the "Superfund" law.[176] The committees requested documents relating to a number of on-going enforcement actions from EPA Administrator Anne Gorsuch Burford. The documents sought included memoranda of EPA and DOJ attorneys containing litigation and negotiation strategy, settlement positions, and other similar materials.[177] After Ms. Burford's initial refusal, the subcommittees issued subpoenas but compliance was resisted on the grounds that the documents requested were "enforcement sensitive" and were part of open law enforcement files. At the direction of President Reagan, Ms. Burford claimed executive privilege to prevent their disclosure.

The House Transportation Subcommittee acted first, citing Ms. Burford for contempt of Congress, an action that was affirmed by the full Committee. The full House of Representatives voted 259 to 105 to support the contempt citation.[178] The DOJ's first attempted to obtain a federal court order enjoining the House from forwarding the contempt citation to the U.S. Attorney for prosecution pursuant to the criminal contempt statute (discussed in depth in the next section), but failed.[179] Following a brief period of negotiation with the Public Works and Transportation Committee, DOJ reached an agreement for release of the documents. The documents were released to the subcommittee in stages, beginning first with briefings and redacted copies, and eventually ending with unredacted copies that could only be examined by committee members and up to two designated committee staffers.[180]

The Chairman of the House Energy and Commerce Committee, Representative John Dingell, refused to accept the agreement between the DOJ and the House Public Works and Transportation Committee given its limitations on access and time delays. After a threat to issue new subpoenas and pursue a further contempt citation, negotiations were resumed. The result was an agreement that all documents covered by the initial subpoena would be delivered to the subcommittee. There were to be no briefings and no multi-stage process of redacted documents leading to unredacted documents.[181] The subcommittee agreed to handle all "enforcement sensitive" documents in executive session, giving them confidential treatment.[182] The subcommittee, however, reserved for itself the right to release the documents or use them in public session, after providing "reasonable notice" to the EPA.[183] If the EPA did not agree, the documents would not be released or used in public session unless the chairman and ranking minority Member concurred. If they did not concur, the subcommittee could vote on the release of documents and their subsequent use in a public session. Staff access was to be decided by the chairman and ranking minority Member. The agreement was signed by Chairman Dingell, Ranking Member James T. Broyhill, and White House Counsel Fred F. Fielding on March 9, 1983.[184]

Burford II: The Investigation of the Claim of Presidential Privilege

After the House voted to hold Burford in contempt of Congress, the Department, in the name of the United States, filed an unprecedented legal action against the House. The DOJ attempted to obtain to obtain a judicial declaration that Burford had acted lawfully in refusing to comply with the subpoena. Ultimately, the lawsuit was dismissed,[185] the documents were provided to Congress, and the contempt citation was dropped. However, a number of questions about the role of the Department during the controversy remained: whether the Department, not the EPA, had made the decision to persuade the President to assert executive privilege; whether the Department had directed the U.S. Attorney for the District of Columbia not to present the Burford contempt citation to the grand jury for prosecution and had made the decision to sue the House; and, generally, whether there was a conflict of interest in the Department's simultaneously advising the President, representing Burford, investigating alleged executive branch wrongdoing, and enforcing the congressional criminal contempt statute. These and related questions raised by the Department's actions were the subject of an investigation by the House Judiciary Committee beginning in early 1983. The committee issued a final report on its investigation in December 1985.[186]

Although the Judiciary Committee ultimately was able to obtain access to virtually all of the documentation and other information it sought from the Department, in many respects this investigation proved as contentious as the earlier EPA controversy from which it arose. In its final report, the committee concluded that

> [T]he Department of Justice, through many of the same senior officials who were most involved in the EPA controversy, consciously prevented the Judiciary Committee from obtaining information in the Department's possession that was essential to the Committee's inquiry into the Department's role in that controversy. Most notably, the Department deliberately, and without advising the Committee, withheld a massive volume of vital handwritten notes and chronologies for over one year. These materials, which the Department knew came within the Committee's February 1983 document request, contained the bulk of the relevant documentary information about the Department's activities outlined in this report and provided a basis for many of the Committee's findings.[187]

Among the other abuses cited by the committee were the withholding of a number of other relevant documents until the committee had independently learned of their existence,[188] as well as materially "false and misleading" testimony before the committee by the head of the Department's Office of Legal Counsel.[189]

The committee's initial request for documentation was contained in a February 1983 letter from its chairman, Representative Peter Rodino, to Attorney General William French Smith. The committee requested that the Department "supply all documents prepared by or in the possession of the Department in any way relating to the withholding of documents that Congressional committees have subpoenaed from the EPA."[190] The letter also specifically requested, among other things, a narrative description of the activities of each division or other unit of the Department relating to the withholding of the EPA materials, information about the Department's apparent conflict of interest in simultaneously advising the executive branch while being responsible for prosecuting the Burford contempt citation, and any instructions given by the Department to the U.S. Attorney not to present the Burford contempt to a grand jury.

At first, the Department provided only publicly available documents in response to this and other document requests from the committee.[191] However, after a series of meetings between committee staff and senior Department officials, an agreement was reached whereby committee staff were permitted to review the materials responsive to these requests at the Department to determine which documents the committee would need for its inquiry.[192] Committee staff reviewed thousands of documents from the Land and Natural Resources Division, the Civil Division, the Office of Legal Counsel, the Office of Legislative Affairs, the Office of Public Affairs, and the offices of the Attorney General, the Deputy Attorney General, and the Solicitor General.[193]

In July 1983, the committee chairman wrote to the Attorney General requesting copies of 105 documents that committee staff identified during review as particularly important to the committee's inquiry.[194] By May 1984, only a few of those documents had been provided to the committee, and the chairman again wrote to the Attorney General requesting the Department's cooperation in the investigation. In that letter, the chairman advised the Attorney General that the committee's preliminary investigation had raised serious questions of misconduct, including potential criminal misconduct, in the Department's decision to withhold EPA documents.[195] The committee finally received 105 documents in July 1984, a full year after it had initially requested access. At that time, the committee also obtained the written notes and a number of other documents that had been earlier withheld.[196]

There was also disagreement about the access committee staff would have to interview Department employees. The Department demanded that it be permitted to have one or more Department attorneys present at each interview. The committee feared that the presence of Department representatives might intimidate the Department employees in their interviews and stated that it was willing to permit a Department representative to be present only if the representative was "walled-off" from Department officials involved with the controversy, if the substance of interviews was not revealed to subsequent interviewees, and if employees could be interviewed without a Department representative present if so requested. The Department ultimately agreed to permit the interviews to go forward without its attorneys present. If a Department employee requested representation, the Department employed private counsel for that purpose. In all, committee staff interviewed 26 current and former Department employees, including four Assistant Attorneys general, under this agreement.[197]

Partly as a result of these interviews, as well as from information in the handwritten notes that had been initially withheld, the committee concluded that it also required access to Criminal Division documents about the origins of the criminal investigation of former EPA Assistant Administrator Rita Lavelle. The committee needed these documents to determine if the Department had considered instituting the investigation to obstruct the committee's inquiry. The committee also requested information about the Department's earlier withholding of the handwritten notes and other documents to determine whether Department officials had deliberately withheld the documents in an attempt to obstruct the committee's investigation.[198] The Department at first refused to provide the committee with documents relating to its Lavelle investigation, citing its withholding as "[c]onsistent with the longstanding practice of the Department not to provide access to active criminal files."[199] The Department also refused to provide the committee with access to documentation related to the Department's handling of the committee's inquiry, objecting to the committee's "ever-broadening scope of ... inquiry."[200]

The committee chairman wrote the Attorney General and objected that the Department was denying the committee access even though no claim of executive privilege had been asserted.[201]

The chairman also maintained that "[i]n this case, of course, no claim of executive privilege could lie because of the interest of the committee in determining whether the documents contain evidence of misconduct by executive branch officials."[202] With respect to the documents relating to the Department's handling of the committee inquiry, the chairman demanded that the Department prepare a detailed index of the withheld documents that included the title, date, and length of each document; its author and all who had seen it; a summary of its contents; an explanation of why it was being withheld; a certification that it contained no evidence of misconduct; and a certification that the Department intended to recommend the President assert executive privilege over it.[203]

With respect to the Lavelle documents, the chairman narrowed the committee's request to "predicate" documents relating to the opening of the investigation and prosecution of Lavelle, as opposed to FBI and other investigative reports reflecting actual investigative work conducted after the opening of the investigation.[204] In response, more than three months after the committee's initial request, the Department produced those two categories of materials.[205]

E.F. Hutton Investigation

In 1985 and 1986, the Crime Subcommittee of the House Judiciary Committee conducted an investigation to determine why no individuals were charged in connection with an investigation of E.F. Hutton, an American stock brokerage firm that pled guilty to 2,000 felony counts.[206] As part of this investigation, the subcommittee sought letters to Hutton employees promising not to prosecute, draft indictments, and internal DOJ communications regarding proposals discussing the disposition of charges against Hutton employees.[207] Assistant Attorney General Trott responded to the request by stating:

> We understand this to be a request for prospective memoranda.... It now appears that there is one document prepared early in the investigation that may fall within your request. We will produce that for the Subcommittee after appropriate redactions have been made. We believe that the necessary redactions are those principally set out in *In re Grand Jury Investigation (Lance)*.[208] Thus, such information as the identity of witnesses who testified before the grand jury and the substance of their testimony and the identity of documents which were subpoenaed by the grand jury must be redacted."[209]

The Justice Department also recommended that the subcommittee go to court to obtain access to all of the information, including that which could not be released under the Federal Rules of Criminal Procedure Rule 6(e).[210] The Justice Department went to court to seek guidance regarding the applicability of Rule 6(e) to the documents sought by the subcommittee. In court, the Justice Department argued only on 6(e) grounds, and never claimed that any documents should be withheld on deliberative process grounds. The court dismissed the case because it presented no case or controversy. However, the court did express "serious doubt" as to the applicability of Rule 6(e) to the documents sought by the subcommittee.

The Subcommittee report includes as exhibits a number of deliberative prosecutorial documents. One 21-page memorandum contains a detailed discussion of Hutton's money management practices, and concludes that "these money management techniques violated numerous federal criminal statutes and, therefore, prosecution is appropriate and recommended."[211] The Subcommittee was also provided with a series of memoranda prepared by a line attorney, which analyzed the defenses that could be offered by Hutton officers and the DOJ's responses to those defenses. These memoranda are among many examples of deliberative prosecutorial memoranda provided to the investigating congressional committee by DOJ.[212]

Iran-Contra

In the late 1980s, an intense congressional investigation focused, in part, on Attorney General Edwin Meese's conduct during the Iran-Contra scandal. The House and Senate created their Iran-Contra committees in January 1987. The Iran-Contra Committees demanded the production of the Justice Department's files. Assistant Attorney General John Bolton responded to this request, on behalf of Attorney General Meese, by attempting to withhold the documents by asserting that disclosure would prejudice the pending or anticipated litigation by the Independent Counsel. The Iran-Contra Committees disputed that contention, required the production of all Justice Department documents, and questioned all knowledgeable Justice Department officers up to, and including, Attorney General Meese.

One major aspect of the Iran-Contra Committees' investigation focused on the inadequacies of the so-called "Meese Inquiry," the team led by Attorney General Meese that examined the National Security Council (NSC) staff in late November 1987. The Iran-Contra Committees concluded that this inquiry had the effect of forewarning the NSC staff to shred their records and fix upon an agreed false story, ending any opportunity to uncover the obscured aspects of the scandal. The congressional investigation provided documentary evidence regarding incompetence, at best, by the Attorney General's team during the Meese Inquiry. The congressional report documented this incompetence, which included the Attorney General taking no notes and remembering no details of his crucial interviews of CIA Director Casey and others; the DOJ inquiry taking no steps to secure the remaining unshredded documents; and the Justice Department team allowing the documents to be shredded while the team was in the room. Furthermore, the inquiry team excluded the Criminal Division and the FBI from the case until it was too late.[213]

Rocky Flats Environmental Crimes Plea Bargain

In June 1992 the Subcommittee on Investigations and Oversight of the House Committee on Science, Space, and Technology commenced a review of the DOJ-negotiated plea bargain settlement in the investigation and prosecution of Rockwell International Corporation. Rockwell was accused of committing environmental crimes in its capacity as manager and operating contractor of the Department of Energy's (DOE) Rocky Flats nuclear weapons facility.[214]

The settlement was the culmination of a five-year investigation, conducted by a joint government task force involving the FBI, the DOJ, the Environmental Protection Agency (EPA), the EPA's National Enforcement Investigation Centers, and the DOE Inspector General. The subcommittee was concerned by several details, including with the size of the settlement fine relative to the profits made by the contractor and the damage caused by inappropriate activities; the lack of personal indictments of either Rockwell or DOE personnel despite a DOJ finding that the crimes were "institutional crimes" that "were the result of a culture, substantially encouraged and nurtured by DOE, where environmental compliance was a much lower priority than the production and recovery of plutonium and the manufacture of nuclear 'triggers'"; and that reimbursements provided by the government to Rockwell for expenses in the cases and the contractual arrangements between Rockwell and DOE may have created disincentives for environmental compliance and aggressive prosecution of the case.

The subcommittee held ten days of hearings, seven in executive session, in which it took testimony from the U.S. Attorney for the District of Colorado; an assistant U.S. Attorney for the District of Colorado; a DOJ line attorney from Main Justice; and an FBI field agent; it also received voluminous FBI field investigative reports, interview summaries, and documents submitted to the grand jury not subject to Rule 6(e).[215]

At one point in the proceedings all the witnesses who were under subpoena, upon written instructions from the Acting Assistant Attorney General for the Criminal Division, refused to answer questions concerning internal deliberations in which decisions were made about the investigation and prosecution of Rockwell, the DOE, and their employees. Two of the witnesses advised that they had information on these matters and, but for the DOJ directive, would have answered the subcommittee's inquiries. The subcommittee members unanimously authorized the chairman to send a letter to President George H. W. Bush requesting that he either personally assert executive privilege as the basis for directing the witnesses to withhold the information or direct DOJ to retract its instructions to the witnesses. The President took neither course and the DOJ subsequently reiterated its position that the information sought would chill Department personnel. The subcommittee then moved to hold the U.S. Attorney in contempt of Congress.

A last minute agreement forestalled the contempt citation. Under the agreement DOJ had to issue a new instruction to all personnel under subpoena to answer all questions put to them by the subcommittee, including those which related to internal deliberations with respect to the plea bargain. Those instructions were also to apply to all Department witnesses, including FBI personnel, who might testify in the future. Additionally, transcripts were to be made of all interviews and provided to the witnesses. They were not to be made public except to the extent they needed to be used to refresh the recollection or impeach the testimony of other witnesses called before the subcommittee in a public hearing. Witnesses were to be interviewed by staff under oath. Finally, the subcommittee reserved the right to hold further hearings in the future at which time it could call other Department witnesses who would be instructed not to invoke the deliberative process privilege as a reason for not answering subcommittee questions.[216]

Investigation of the Justice Department's Environmental Crimes Section

From 1992 to 1994, the House Commerce Committee's Subcommittee on Oversight and Investigations conducted an extensive investigation into the impact of the DOJ on the effectiveness of the EPA's criminal enforcement program. The probe involved two public hearings, nearly three years of staff work, intensive review of documents (many of which were obtained only though subpoenas), and the effort to overcome persistent DOJ resistance. The investigation focused on allegations of mismanagement of the Environmental Crimes Section (ECS), a division of DOJ charged with environmental prosecution responsibilities. It also examined DOJ's decision to centralize control of environmental prosecution in ECS, in Washington, while simultaneously decentralizing other areas of prosecutorial contrail and how this impacted the relationship between ECS and U.S. Attorney's offices.

The Subcommittee's investigation was delayed for months by DOJ's refusal to cooperate with requests for interviews and documents. The initial phase of the investigation required overcoming refusals to produce internal EPA documents bearing on 17 closed criminal environmental cases. The documents ultimately produced by EPA included Reports of Investigation, case agent notes, internal reports and memoranda, communications with private parties, and correspondence with DOJ. The next phase concentrated on attempts to obtain staff interviews with DOJ line attorneys with first-hand information on whether various closed cases had been mishandled, including three Assistant U.S. Attorneys. DOJ officials initially refused, arguing that allowing access would have a chilling effect on Department officials and noting the Department's historic reluctance to comply with such requests. Instead, it offered to provide access to the head of ECS instead. The Subcommittee responded that it was premature to interview the ECS head without interviewing line attorneys who had first hand knowledge of the facts in question. The change of administration in 1993 did not result in an easing of DOJ's resistant posture and in May 1993 the Subcommittee voted to issue 26 subpoenas to present and former DOJ attorneys. In June 1993 DOJ acquiesced to staff interviews of the subpoenaed attorneys pursuant to a negotiated agreement. Document subpoenas were also authorized but not issued. However, continued refusal to produce the documents voluntarily resulted in issuance of document subpoenas in March 1994 to the Attorney General and the Acting Assistant Attorney General for the Environment and Natural Resources Division. Some of these documents involved closed cases, but DOJ claimed they were "deliberative" in nature and that only limited access could be allowed. Other documents withheld involved internal DOJ communications about responses to the Subcommittee's investigation after the six cases were closed. At the time the subpoenas were served, the Acting Assistant Attorney General's nomination for the position was before the Senate Judiciary Committee. The chairman of the Subcommittee advised the Judiciary Committee of the withholding and a hold was put on her nomination. In late March, DOJ agreed to comply with the subpoena and the documents were provided over a period of months. Coincidentally the Senate hold was lifted.

As a result of the investigation, the policy of centralizing control of environmental prosecutions in Washington, DC was reversed, and control was returned to the U.S. Attorney's offices. Additionally, the ECS top management was replaced.[217]

Ruby Ridge

The next case study, involving the DOJ Office of Professional Responsibility, which monitors the conduct of Department personnel, is notable for its revelations of a number of sensitive, previously undisclosed internal investigations in the face of extraordinary agency resistance. That occurred during the 1995 investigation by the Senate Judiciary Committee's Subcommittee on Terrorism, Technology and Government Information of allegations that several branches of the DOJ and the Department of the Treasury had engaged in serious criminal and professional misconduct in the investigation, apprehension, and prosecution of Randall Weaver and Kevin Harris at Ruby Ridge, Idaho.

The subcommittee held 14 days of hearings in which it heard testimony from 62 witnesses, including DOJ, FBI, and Treasury officials, line attorneys and agents, obtained various internal reports from these agencies,[218] and issued a final report.[219] The subcommittee's hearings revealed that the federal agencies involved conducted at least eight internal investigations into charges of misconduct at Ruby Ridge, none of which had ever been publically released.[220] DOJ expressed reluctance to allow the Subcommittee to see the documents out of a concern they would interfere with the ongoing investigation but ultimately provided some of them under agreed-upon conditions regarding their public release. The most important of those documents was the Report of the Ruby Ridge Task Force.[221] The Task Force was established by the DOJ after the acquittals of Randy Weaver and Kevin Harris of all charges in the killing of a Deputy U.S. Marshal[222] to investigate charges that federal law enforcement agents and federal prosecutors involved in the investigation, apprehension, and prosecution of Weaver and Harris may have engaged in professional misconduct and criminal wrongdoing. The allegations were referred to DOJ's Office of Professional Responsibility (OPR).

The Task Force was headed by an Assistant Counsel from OPR and consisted of four career attorneys from DOJ's Criminal Division and a number of FBI inspectors and investigative agents. The Task Force submitted a 542 page report to OPR on June 10, 1994, which found numerous problems with the conduct of the FBI, the U.S. Marshals Service, and the U.S. Attorneys Office in Idaho, and made recommendations for institutional changes to address the problems it found. It also concluded that portions of the rules of engagement issued by the FBI during the incident were unconstitutional under the circumstances, and that the second of two shots fired by a member of the FBI's Hostage Rescue Team (HRT), which resulted in the death of Vicki Weaver, was not reasonable.

The Task Force recommended that the matter of the shooting be referred to a prosecutorial component of the Department for a determination as to whether a criminal investigation was appropriate. OPR reviewed the Task Force Report and transmitted the Report to the Deputy Attorney General with a memorandum that dissented from the recommendation that the shooting of Vicki Weaver by the HRT member be reviewed for prosecutorial merit based on the view that the agent's actions were not unreasonable considering the totality of the circumstances. The Deputy Attorney General referred the Task Force recommendation for prosecutorial review to the Criminal Section of the Civil Rights Division, which concluded that there was no basis for criminal prosecution.

The Task Force Report was the critical basis for the Subcommittee's inquiries during the hearings and its discussion and conclusions in its final report.[223]

Campaign Finance Investigations

Allegations of violations of campaign finance laws and regulations surfaced during the latter stages of the 1996 presidential election campaign and became the subjects of investigations by committees in both Houses between 1996 and 2000. Several of the committee inquiries focused on the nature and propriety of DOJ actions and non-actions during the course of investigations undertaken by the Department. The following two investigations are illustrative.

In 1997, the Senate Governmental Affairs Committee began an investigation into allegations of improprieties with respect to the flow of money into campaigns, particularly into the Republican and Democratic National Committees, and money from foreign sources. After the first round of hearings, the committee became concerned with the quality of DOJ's prosecution efforts as well as with evidence of a lack of cooperation and coordination between Main Justice and the FBI. In 1999 the committee held hearings on DOJ's handling of the investigation of Yah Lin "Charlie" Trie, an Arkansas native with a long time friendly relationship with President Clinton, who had frequent access to the White House and was alleged to have funneled $220,000 from foreign sources to the Democratic National Committee. Mr. Trie also provided the President's Legal Expense Trust (PLET) with $789,000 in sequentially numbered money orders. During the course of the DOJ investigation, Mr. Trie fled the country, leaving an agent in control of his business. In April 1997, the committee subpoenaed business documents relating to its campaign finance investigation and documents relating to the PLET. At the same time the DOJ's Campaign Finance Task Force was engaged in a parallel investigation. As early as June 1997, FBI Agents in Little Rock became convinced that Trie's agent was destroying subpoenaed documents, a process that continued until October 1997. During that period, the FBI attempted to obtain a search warrant to prevent further document destruction. DOJ Task Force supervisory attorneys declined to grant permission to seek a search warrant, believing there was insufficient probable cause. The committee subpoenaed four FBI special agents who testified about their efforts to procure a search warrant, the Task Force supervisory attorney who refused its issuance, and the Chief of the Public Integrity Section of DOJ. The committee also obtained from DOJ the investigatory notes of the special agents, the draft affidavit in support of the warrant requests, the notes of the Task Force supervisor, and a memo from one of the special agents to FBI Director Freeh expressing concern over DOJ handling of the investigation.[224]

In December 1997, press reports indicated that FBI Director Freeh had sent a memorandum to Attorney General Reno suggesting that she seek appointment of an independent counsel to conduct the campaign finance investigation in order to avoid the appearance of a political conflict of interest.[225] The House Committee on Government Reform and Oversight scheduled a hearing and requested that Freeh appear and produce the memo. The Attorney General intervened and explained that she would not comply, citing longstanding DOJ policy prohibiting disclosure of deliberative material in open criminal cases to Congress and concerns about the chilling effect such disclosures would have on Department personnel in future investigations. The Committee issued subpoenas on December 5, 1997, and both Reno and Freeh refused to comply.

At no time did the Attorney General make a formal claim of executive privilege. In July 1998 the committee learned that the head of DOJ's Campaign Finance Task Force, Charles La Bella, had prepared a lengthy memorandum for the Attorney General, which concluded that the Attorney General was required by both the mandatory and discretionary provisions of the independent counsel law to appoint an independent counsel. On July 24, 1998, the Committee issued a subpoena for both the Freeh and La Bella memos. The Attorney General refused compliance again and on August 6, 1998, the committee voted to hold the Attorney General in contempt of Congress.[226] However, the contempt report was not taken up on the House floor prior to the end of the 105th Congress.

On May 2000, following press reports indicating that the La Bella memo had been leaked in its entirety to a newspaper, the Committee again subpoenaed the memos.[227]

The Attorney General still refused to release the memos but offered to allow committee staff to review unredacted copies without taking any notes. Negotiations continued while the committee began review under the DOJ conditions.

Ultimately, an accommodation was reached in which all subpoenaed memoranda were to be produced to the committee. The documents would be kept in a secure facility with access restricted to a limited number of staff. The committee agreed to give DOJ notice in advance if it intended to release the documents and to allow DOJ to argue its case against disclosure. The committee notified the Attorney General of its intent to release the documents at a June 6 hearing.[228] The memos were released to the public on that date by unanimous consent.[229]

Misuse of Informants in the FBI's Boston Regional Office

In early 2001, the House Committee on Government Reform commenced an investigation on FBI corruption in its Boston Regional office that encompassed events extending back to the mid-1960s. After continued refusal to cooperate with requests for documents, the committee issued a subpoena on September 6, 2001 for a number of prosecution and declination memoranda about DOJ's investigation of the handling of confidential informants in New England.[230] DOJ officials made it clear that they would not comply. In December 2001, the committee renewed its request for the subpoenaed documents after a hearing on the request scheduled for September 13, 2001, was postponed because of the September 11 terrorist attacks.[231] That subpoena sought, among other material, Justice Department documents relating to alleged law enforcement corruption in the FBI's Boston office that occurred over a period of almost 30 years. During that time, FBI officials allegedly knowingly allowed innocent persons to be convicted of murder on the false testimony of a cooperating witness and two informants in order to protect the undercover activities of those informants. Later, the FBI knowingly permitted two other informants to commit some 21 additional murders during the period they acted as informants, and, finally, gave the informants warning of an impending grand jury indictment, which allowed one of them to flee.[232]

The President directed the Attorney General not to release the documents because disclosure "would inhibit the candor necessary to the effectiveness of the deliberative processes by which the Department makes prosecutorial decisions."[233] Additionally, the executive branch argued that committee access to the documents "threatens to politicize the criminal justice process" and to undermine the fundamental purpose of the separation of power doctrine, "which was to protect individual liberty."[234] In defending the assertion of the privilege, the Justice Department claimed it was following a historical policy of withholding deliberative prosecutorial documents from Congress in both open and closed civil and criminal cases.[235] Pending at the time were a number of Federal Tort Claims Act suits brought by the falsely convicted persons and their families, claiming the government knowingly used fabricated testimony to achieve the conviction.

Initial congressional hearings after the privilege claim was made demonstrated the rigidity of the Department's position. The Department later agreed there might be some room for compromise, and on January 10, 2002, White House Counsel Alberto Gonzales wrote to Chairman Burton conceding that it was a "misimpression" that congressional committees could never have access to deliberative documents from a criminal investigation or prosecution. "There is no such bright-line policy, nor did we intend to articulate any such policy."[236] However, he continued, since the documents "sought a very narrow and particularly sensitive category of deliberative matters" and "absent unusual circumstances, the Executive Branch has traditionally protected these highly sensitive deliberative documents against public or congressional disclosure" unless a committee showed a "compelling or specific need" for the documents.[237] The documents continued to be withheld until a February 6, 2002 hearing, when the committee heard expert testimony describing over 30 specific instances since 1920 in which the DOJ disclosed deliberative documents to Congress. These materials included prosecutorial memoranda for both open and closed cases, testimony of subordinate Department employees, such as line attorneys, FBI field agents and U.S. Attorneys, and detailed testimony about specific instances of DOJ's failure to prosecute meritorious cases. In all instances, investigating committees also received documents from open and closed case files, including FBI investigative reports, summaries of FBI interviews, memoranda and correspondence prepared during undercover operations, and documents presented to grand juries not protected by Rule 6(e), among other similar "sensitive materials." Shortly after the hearing the committee was given access to the disputed documents.[238] On July 26, 2007, a Massachusetts federal district court judge awarded the convicted persons and their families $101.7 million under the Federal Tort Claims Act, finding the government liable for malicious prosecution, civil conspiracy, infliction of emotional distress, and negligence.[239]

The committee's final report concluded that the documents withheld from it were indispensable to the success of its investigation and that the claim of executive privilege was part of a pattern of obstruction that impeded its investigation:

> When the FBI Office of Professional Responsibility conducted an investigation of the activities of New England law enforcement, it concluded in 1997: "There is no evidence that prosecutorial discretion was exercised on behalf of informants [James] Bulger and/or [Stephen] Flemmi." This is untrue. Former U.S. Attorney Jeremiah O'Sullivan was asked in the December 5, 2002 committee hearing whether prosecutorial discretion had been exercised on behalf of Bulger and Flemmi and he said that it had. A review of documents in the possession of the Justice Department also confirms this to be true. Had the committee permitted

the assertion of executive privilege by the President to be unchallenged, this information would never have been known. That the Justice Department concluded that prosecutorial discretion had not benefitted Bulger or Flemmi—while at the same time fighting to keep Congress from obtaining information proving this statement to be untrue—is extremely troubling.[240]

Removal and Replacement of United States Attorneys

Commencing in early 2007, the House Judiciary Committee and its Subcommittee on Commercial and Administrative Law and the Senate Judiciary Committee began investigations of the termination and replacement of nine U.S. Attorneys in 2006; The committees sought an explanation of the reasons for the terminations, who was involved in the removal and replacement decisions, and what factors may have influenced the considerations for removal and replacement. During the initial phase of the investigations, DOJ voluntarily made available former and current Department officials and employees for closed door interviews and testimony at hearings. The House subcommittee held five days of hearings,[241] while the full committee held two days of hearings.[242] DOJ witnesses included, among others: the Attorney General, the Deputy Attorney General, the removed U.S. Attorneys, the Chief of Staff to the Deputy Attorney General, the former Chief of Staff to the Attorney General, the acting Associate Attorney General, the Principal Associate Deputy Attorney General, the Deputy Assistant Attorney General and Chief of Staff of the Criminal Division, the Principal Deputy Director of the Executive Office of U.S. Attorneys, the former Director of the Office of U.S. Attorneys and current U.S. Attorney for the Western District of Pennsylvania, the Associate Deputy Attorney General, and the Acting Attorney General for New Mexico.

On the basis of the witness testimony and records produced by the DOJ, the committees turned their attention to the role the White House played in the removals and sought similar voluntary provision of witnesses and documents. The White House Counsel responded by offering the committees limited availability to some documents and limited access to witnesses in closed sessions, but without any transcripts of the interviews and with limited permissible questions. As a condition of this proposal the committees had to commit in advance not to subsequently pursue any additional White House-related information by any other means, regardless of what the initial review of documents might reveal.

After failing to procure White House documents and witnesses on a voluntary basis, on June 13, 2007, the chairman of the House and Senate committee issued subpoenas to Joshua Bolten, the White House Chief of Staff (as custodian of the White House Documents) for relevant White House documents, returnable on June 28, 2007. On that date, the House committee chairman issued a subpoena for documents and testimony to former White House Counsel Harriet Meirs, returnable on July 12, 2007 and the Senate committee chairman issued a similar subpoena to former White House Political Director Sara Taylor, returnable on July 11, 2007. The White House Counsel thereafter announced that Mr. Bolten would not produce any documents on the basis of a presidential claim of executive privilege and that no privilege logs would be provided. Furthermore, he announced the Ms. Miers had been directed not to appear at the hearing at all based on the notion that the privilege assertion cloaked a witness with "absolute immunity" from even appearing in response to a subpoena.[243] On the return dates of the subpoenas, Ms. Miers did not appear and Mr. Bolten did not produce the subpoenaed documents.

On July 12, the House subcommittee voted 7-5 to hold Ms. Miers in contempt of Congress, and on July 19, Mr. Bolten was held in contempt by the subcommittee by a 7-3 vote. On July 25, both Ms. Miers and Mr. Bolten were held in contempt by the full House Judiciary Committee by a vote of 21-17.[244] The full House of Representatives voted to hold Ms. Miers and Mr. Bolten in contempt of Congress on February 14, 2008, by a vote of 223-32.[245] The House passed one resolution, H.Res. 982 that incorporated two other resolutions, H.Res. 979 and 982. H.Res. 979 provided that the Speaker of the House shall certify the contempt of the House report to the U.S. Attorney for the District of Columbia for presentation of the matter to a grand jury. H.Res. 980 authorized the Chairman of the House Judiciary Committee to initiate a civil action in federal district court to seek declaratory and injunctive relief "affirming the duty of any individual to comply with any subpoena."

Upon submission of the certified report to the U.S. Attorney by the Speaker, the Attorney General announced that because Ms. Miers and Mr. Bolten were acting pursuant to direct orders of the President, he had determined that their refusals to comply with the subpoenas did not constitute a crime, and that the contempt citation would not be presented for grand jury action.[246] With criminal enforcement foreclosed, the Committee filed a civil action on March 10, 2008 seeking a declaratory judgment and injunctive relief to enforce the subpoena. On July 31, 2008, the District Court granted the Committee's motion for partial summary judgment, declaring that "Ms. Miers is not absolutely immune from congressional process"[247] and that "she must appear before the Committee to provide testimony" when faced with a duly issued congressional subpoena.[248] It ordered Ms. Miers and Mr. Bolten to "produce all non-privileged documents required by the applicable subpoenas and... provide to [the Committee] a specific description of the documents withheld from production on the basis of executive privilege consistent with the terms of the Memorandum Opinion issued on this date."[249]

CIA Agent Identity Leak

In July 2003, Robert D. Novak wrote a column revealing the identity of Valerie Plame Wilson—a covert CIA agent. His column appeared shortly after Ms. Plame's husband, former U.S. ambassador Joseph Wilson, criticized the Bush Administration for claiming that Saddam Hussein bought uranium from Niger. This sequence sparked an FBI investigation into whether White House officials had illegally disclosed Ms. Plame's identity in retaliation for Mr. Wilson's remarks. On March 6, 2007, I. Lewis "Scooter" Libby, Vice President Cheney's Chief of Staff, was convicted of perjury, obstruction of justice, and making a false statement to federal investigators concerning the leak. During the criminal investigation, Special Counsel Patrick J. Fitzgerald interviewed Vice President Dick Cheney, President Bush, and other senior White House officials about the incident. Mr. Libby's trial raised a number of questions concerning their role in the affair. Following its conclusion, the House Oversight and Government Reform Committee (the "Committee") launched an investigation into the disclosure, aiming to discover: "(1) How did such a serious violation of our national security occur? (2) Did the White House take the appropriate investigative and disciplinary steps after the breach occurred? And (3) what changes in White House procedures are necessary to prevent future violations of our national security from occurring?"[250]

On July 16, 2007, Henry Waxman, Chairman of the Committee, requested that Mr. Fitzgerald produce all information from his investigation relevant to answering these questions.[251] On January 18, 2008, the Department of Justice permitted the review of redacted interviews with White House staff, but argued that separation of powers and confidentiality concerns barred access to reports detailing interviews with the President and Vice President.[252] The Committee's analysis of these staff interview reports raised more questions about Vice President Cheney's role in the affair. On June 3, 2008, Chairman Waxman wrote to Attorney General Michael Mukasey, again requesting access to reports of interviews with the President and Vice President. On June 11, 2008, the Justice Department again refused.[253] The next day, the Committee issued a subpoena to the Attorney General, demanding the production of unredacted "transcripts, reports, notes, and other documents relating to interviews outside the presence of a grand jury" the President and Vice President.[254]

On June 24, 2008, the Justice Department responded that it would not release reports of interviews with the President or Vice President. It indicated it was willing to "discuss ... the possibility" of permitting more expansive review of previously redacted portions of interviews with White House staff, but the "confidentiality interests" of interviews with the President and Vice President were of a "greater constitutional magnitude"[255] that had not been overcome. These reports dealt with "internal White House deliberations and communications relating to foreign policy and national security ... the absolute core of executive privilege."[256] In addition, the subpoena implicated "separation of powers concern[s] relating to the integrity and effectiveness of future law enforcement investigations."[257] The Justice Department argued that revealing records of interviews officials voluntarily participated in to Congress would deter future White House cooperation with criminal investigations, because subsequent Administrations might "limit the scope" of their participation, or simply refuse to be interviewed so as to prevent possible future disclosure to Congress.[258]

Chairman Waxman responded on July 8, 2008, agreeing to refrain from pursuing the interview with President Bush, but reiterating his demand for access to Vice President Cheney's interview and unredacted versions of interviews with White House staff. He noted that at the close of Mr. Libby's trial, Special Prosecutor Fitzgerald remarked that there was a "cloud over what the Vice President did [in connection with the leak]."[259] The interviews with the Vice President were essential in order to investigate this cloud and perform oversight of the executive branch's handling of national security secrets. Waxman also rejected the Justice Department's various arguments for withholding the interview reports. First, he argued that no "confidentiality interests" applied since the Vice President knew the interview could be made public when it was conducted and executive privilege was unavailable for "communications voluntarily disclosed outside the White House."[260] Second, he noted that the reports in question did not concern vital national security or foreign policy issues, but were limited to the role the Vice President and others played in leaking national security secrets. Third, he argued the presidential communications privilege was limited to "communications ... with the President or certain advisers directly on his behalf about presidential decisionmaking," and was therefore inapplicable to conversations between the Vice President and his staff.[261] Fourth, President Bush and Vice President Cheney agreed to be interviewed even though similar interviews with the previous Administration had been released. If the risk of this disclosure did not deter them, it would probably not deter future Administrations. Finally, Chairman Waxman informed the Attorney General that the Committee would consider a resolution on July 16 to hold him in contempt of Congress if he did not comply with the subpoena.

On July 16, 2008, the Department of Justice notified the Committee that the President had formally asserted executive privilege over the relevant documents.[262] A July 15, 2008, letter from the Attorney General to the President outlined the legal basis for this claim. The Attorney General argued that the "core" purpose of the executive privilege doctrine was to "preserve[] the confidentiality of internal White House deliberations," and it extended to all executive branch deliberations, "even when the deliberations do not directly implicate presidential decisionmaking."[263] Based on this interpretation, he argued that the subpoenaed documents fell within the presidential communications and deliberative process aspects of executive privilege because they described internal deliberations among staff about how best to advise the President. In addition, the Attorney General maintained that a subpoena for "criminal investigative files" implicated "the law enforcement component of executive privilege," and disclosure to Congress would hamper future White House cooperation with criminal investigations.[264] In order to overcome an executive privilege claim, the letter continued, a committee must point to a "specific legislative decision" that required access to these documents.[265] In his opinion, the Committee's "generalized interest" in the details of the affair did not overcome this standard.[266] At the scheduled contempt hearing on July 16, 2008, Chairman Waxman postponed the vote in order to allow the Committee members to consider the President's claim of executive privilege. On August 5, 2008, the Committee requested a specific description of the documents subject to the President's assertion of executive privilege.[267] Neither the Justice Department nor the Bush Administration responded and no further action was taken before the expiration of the 110th Congress. On August 25, 2008, the Citizens for Responsibility and Ethics in Washington (CREW) brought a FOIA action in a federal district court seeking release of the records. During the next Administration—in October 2009—the court allowed many portions of the records to be withheld in order to protect the deliberative process and presidential communications privileges, as well as national security interests. However, it ruled that the government's chilling effect argument was not sufficient to justify "withhold[ing] the records in their entirety" because the existence of future investigations was "speculative."[268]

Operation Fast and Furious

In early 2011, the Committee on Oversight and Government Reform began investigating the Bureau of Alcohol, Tobacco, Firearms, and Explosives (ATF), a DOJ sub-agency, regarding Operation Fast and Furious—an ATF operation based in the Phoenix, Arizona field office.[269] The investigations were principally triggered by ATF whistleblowers who had alleged that suspected straw purchasers were allowed to amass large quantities of firearms as part of long-term gun trafficking investigations.[270] As a consequence, some of these firearms were allegedly "walked," or trafficked to gunrunners and other criminals in Mexico.[271] In December 2010, two of these firearms were reportedly found at the scene of a shootout near the U.S.-Mexico border where U.S. Border Patrol Agent Brian Terry had been killed.[272] On January 27, 2011, Senator Charles Grassley requested information from ATF Acting Director Kenneth Melson about the "sanctioned ... sale of hundreds of assault weapons to suspected straw purchasers, who then allegedly transported these weapons throughout the southwestern border area and into Mexico."[273] On February 4, 2011, Assistant Attorney General Ronald Weich replied in a letter that the "allegation... that ATF 'sanctioned' or otherwise knowingly allowed the sale of assault weapons to a straw purchaser who then transported them into Mexico—is false."[274]

On March 16, 2011, alerted by numerous independent sources about a "gunwalking" operation, the House Oversight and Government Reform Committee issued a letter to Mr. Melson requesting all documents and communications regarding Operation Fast and Furious. On March 30, 2011, the Department of Justice notified the Committee that it would not provide any of the requested materials. The next day, the Committee issued a subpoena to Mr. Melson for the relevant documents. Over the next few months, the Department produced numerous redacted files but refrained from disclosing "documents that contain detailed information about ... investigative activities ... includ[ing] information that would identify investigative subjects, sensitive techniques, anticipated actions, and other details that would assist individuals in evading our law enforcement efforts."[275] On October 11, 2011, the Justice Department announced that it had concluded its efforts to respond to the subpoena. The Department explained that the disclosure of a "vast majority of withheld material [was] prohibited by statute," while other documents were withheld in order to protect "pending criminal investigations and prosecutions."[276] In addition, "internal communications" concerning the Department's response to the investigation were withheld because "disclosure would implicate substantial Executive Branch confidentiality interests and separation of powers principles"—their release would have a "chilling effect" on future "deliberations."

In response, on October 12, 2011, the Committee subpoenaed Attorney General Eric Holder for an extensive list of materials and communications relating to Operation Fast and Furious, including all documents pertaining to the formulation of the February 4, 2011 letter that denied allegations of "gunwalking." Over the next few months, the Department of Justice produced many documents connected to the program. In a December 2, 2011 letter to the Committee, Deputy Attorney General James Cole admitted that the February 4, 2011 letter "contain[ed] inaccuracies" and "formally withdr[ew]" it.[277] He noted that "Administrations of both political parties" had long agreed that requests for internal deliberation records "implicate[d] significant confidentiality interests grounded in the separation of powers."[278] However, given the "unique circumstances," the Department would "make a rare exception to the Department's recognized protocols and provide ... information related to how the inaccurate information came to be included in the [February 4] letter."[279] The Department still refused to release subpoenaed information in two primary categories: (1) materials judged by the Department not to pertain to the "inappropriate tactics under review by the Committee;"[280] and (2) documents created after the February 4, 2011 letter was issued, relating to "internal communications that were generated in the course of the Department's effort to respond to Congressional and media inquiries."[281] On January 31, 2012, the Committee rejected what it characterized as an attempt to obstruct the congressional investigation, and threatened to hold the Attorney General in contempt if he did not comply fully "with all aspects of the subpoena."[282]

On May 3, 2012, the Committee released a draft version of a contempt report for Committee consideration.[283] It criticized the heavy redaction of many documents and outlined three categories in the subpoena that had not been complied with: (1) information relevant to who at the Justice Department should have known of the tactics used in the program, including documents "relating to the preparation of the wiretap applications;" (2) materials "relating to how officials learned about whistleblowers and what actions they took as a result" in order to reveal "the Department's efforts to slow and otherwise interfere with the Committee's investigation;" and (3) documents pertaining to the Organized Crime Drug Enforcement Task Force in order to "reveal the extent of the lack of information-sharing among DEA, FBI, and ATF."[284] In reply, a May 15, 2012, letter from the Department defended its redactions as necessary to "preserve Department interests" in areas outside the "core of the Committee's review."[285] With respect to category (1) the Department argued it was "prohibited by law" from releasing federal wiretap applications. "[C]ore investigative materials from ... ongoing criminal investigations" were also withheld to protect the "independence and integrity of those efforts," a decision that reflected a long held "non-partisan commitment" to separation of powers principles dating to the "early part of the 19th century."[286] Disclosure, the Department noted, would allow congressional interests to "influence ... the course of the investigation"[287] or "seriously prejudice law enforcement."[288] Turning to category (2) the letter noted that "[a]dministrations of both parties recognized" that "internal communications" made in response to an investigation were "not appropriate for disclosure to the congressional committee conducting the oversight." Additionally, it argued that any release "implicate[d] heightened ... confidentiality interests and ... grave constitutional concerns regarding the separation of powers," including the risk that disclosure would "substantially chill" future deliberations.[289] Finally, it argued that category (3) was sufficiently answered—despite the extremely sensitive "confidentiality" interests at stake—at an October 5, 2011 briefing, where Committee staff were shown redacted version of the relevant files.

On May 18, the Committee agreed to narrow its subpoena to: (1) "information showing the involvement of senior officials during Operation Fast and Furious;" and (2) "documents from after February 4, 2011, related to the Department's response to Congress."[290] After independent whistleblowers provided the Committee with copies of federal wiretap applications, which apparently satisfied its need for information about senior official involvement, the Committee further narrowed its demand to the post-February 4 documents. On June 11, 2012, Chairman Issa announced that the Committee would vote on whether to hold Attorney General Holder in contempt of Congress on June 20, 2012 if he did not comply. On June 14, 2012, the Justice Department indicated it was willing to produce a "subset" of documents from the post-February 4th period, and the Committee replied that their delivery would be sufficient to postpone the contempt vote. However, on June 19, 2012, negotiations collapsed and the document disclosure never materialized.[291]

On June 20, 2012, Deputy Attorney General James Cole informed the Committee that President Obama had claimed executive privilege over the materials. A June 19, 2012, letter from Mr. Holder to President Obama outlined the reasoning behind this assertion.[292] Pointing to past executive privilege claims in similar situations, Mr. Holder argued that it was "well established that ... 'executive privilege ... encompasse[d] Executive Branch deliberative communications,'" and the requested materials "fit squarely within [its] scope."[293] Disclosure, he argued, would "discourage robust and candid deliberations" and "raise 'significant separation of powers concerns,'[294] by 'significantly impair[ing]'[295] the Executive Branch's ability to respond independently and effectively to matters under congressional review." He continued, arguing that a congressional "power to request information ... and then review the ensuing ... discussions regarding how to respond to that request would ... 'introduce a significantly unfair imbalance to the oversight process.'"[296] Holder also identified an "additional, particularized separation of powers concern" invoked here because the Committee "sought information about ongoing criminal investigations and prosecutions. Such information would itself be protected by executive privilege." In order for a congressional committee subpoena to overcome an executive privilege claim, the letter continued, it must show that the relevant documents are "demonstrably critical"[297] to a "legitimate legislative responsibilit[y]."[298] Mr. Holder argued that in light of the Committee's rejection of the Department's "recent[] offering to provide the Committee with a briefing, based on documents that the Committee could retain" that would cover the post-February 4 period, the "purported connection between the congressional interest cited and the documents at issue is now highly attenuated."[299] As a result, there was no "'demonstrably critical' need for further access to the Department's deliberations."[300] Finally, the Department argued that the "'only informing function' constitutionally vested in Congress 'is that of informing itself about subjects susceptible to legislation, not that of informing the public.'"[301] While the Committee was entitled to the documents previously released—regarding what Department officials knew of the Operation—the Committee had failed to show "*any* particularized interest ... let alone a need that would further a legislative function" for "other aspects of the Department's response to congressional and related media inquiries, such as procedures or strategies for responding to the Committee's requests."[302]

On June 20, 2012, the Committee approved a contempt of Congress resolution along party lines against Mr. Holder with a 23-17 vote. The contempt citation was reported to the full House, and on June 28, 2012, two important resolutions were passed. The first, H.Res. 711, constituted the formal criminal contempt citation and was approved by a vote of 255-67.[303] The resolution found the Attorney General in contempt of Congress for his failure to comply with a congressional subpoena and directed the Speaker, pursuant to 2 U.S.C. §194, to certify the contempt citation to the U.S. Attorney for the District of Columbia for prosecution. The second resolution, H.Res. 706, authorized Chairman Issa to initiate a judicial proceeding on behalf of the Committee "to seek declaratory judgments affirming the duty of Eric H. Holder Jr....to comply with any subpoena...issued to him by the Committee as part of its investigation into [Operation Fast and Furious]."[304] H.Res. 706 was approved by a vote of 258-95.[305]

Consistent with DOJ's legal position and the precedent set in the previous contempt actions,[306] Deputy Attorney General James Cole informed Speaker Boehner on the same day that the contempt was approved that "the [DOJ] has determined that the Attorney General's response to the subpoena issued by the Committee on Oversight and Government Reform does not constitute a crime, and therefore the Department will not bring the congressional contempt citation before a grand jury or take any other action to prosecute the Attorney General."[307]

Although the criminal prosecution of the Attorney General for contempt of Congress appeared to be then foreclosed, the Committee still exercised the authority granted to be in H.Res. 706 and filed a civil enforcement action on August 13, 2012. The case will not resolve whether DOJ has an obligation to prosecute contempt citations that have been approved by a House of Congress and forwarded to the appropriate U.S. Attorney. Nor is it likely that the court will opine on the scope of the contempt power and its proper application. Instead, if the court proceeds to the merits of the claim, the case will likely focus only on the validity of the Committee subpoenas. In evaluating whether the Attorney General is required to comply with the subpoena, the court will likely consider whether the subject matter covered by the subpoena was within the Committee's jurisdiction and whether the Committee was pursuing a valid legislative purpose.[308] Perhaps more significantly, the court will also likely consider whether the documents in question were properly protected by executive privilege, and if so, whether the Committee's need for those documents supersedes that privilege.[309] The case is currently pending before the U.S. District Court for the District of Columbia.[310]

End Notes

[1] See generally CRS Report RL30240, Congressional Oversight Manual, by Todd Garvey et al., (June 10, 2011) at 5- 17, 87-108, 114-40 [hereinafter Oversight Manual].

[2] Id. at 2-4.

[3] See Todd David Peterson, Congressional Oversight of Open Criminal Investigations, 77 NOTRE DAME L. REV. 1373, 1410-11 (2002).

[4] See Roberto Iraola, Congressional Oversight, Executive Privilege, and Requests for Information Relating to Federal Criminal Investigations and Prosecutions, 87 IOWA L. REV. 1559, 1594-95 (2002).

[5] United States v. Am. Tel. & Tel. Co., 551 F.2d 384 (D.C. Cir. 1976) [hereinafter AT&T]; Senate Select Comm. on Presidential Campaign Activities v. Nixon, 498 F.2d 725 (D.C. Cir. 1974) [hereinafter Senate Select Committee]; Miers, 558 F.Supp.2d 53; United States v. House of Representatives of U.S., 556 F. Supp. 150 (D.D.C. 1983) [hereinafter House of Representatives].

[6] Senate Select Committee, 498 F.2d 725; Miers, 558 F. Supp. 2d 53.

[7] See, e.g., Nixon v. Administrator of General Services, 433 U.S. 435 (1977); Eastland v. United States Servicemen's Fund, 421 U.S. 491 (1975); Barenblatt v. United States, 360 U.S. 109 (1959); Watkins v. United States, 354 U.S. 178 (1957); McGrain v. Daugherty, 273 U.S. 135 (1927).

[8] 421 U.S. at 504 n.15 (quoting Barenblatt, 360 U.S. at 111).

[9] 354 U.S. at 187.

[10] Id.

[11] Id. at 182.

[12] Id. at 200 n.33.

[13] Kilbourn v. Thompson, 103 U.S. 168, 204 (1880).

[14] Watkins, 354 U.S. at 187.

[15] See, e.g., McGrain, 273 U.S. 135; see also In Re Chapman, 166 U.S. 661 (1897).

[16] 103 U.S. 168 (1881).

[17] McGrain, 273 U.S. 135; see also Townsend v. United States, 95 F.2d 352 (D.C. Cir. 1938); LEADING CASES ON CONGRESSIONAL INVESTIGATORY POWER 7 (Comm. Print 1976) [hereinafter Leading Cases]. For a different assessment of foundational case law concerning the requirement of a legislative purpose, see Allen B. Moreland, Congressional Investigations and Private Persons, 40 SO. CAL. L. REV. 189, 232 (1967).

[18] 166 U.S. 661, 669 (1897).

[19] In re Chapman, 166 U.S. at 699.

[20] 273 U.S. 135 (1927).

[21] See Appendix section "Teapot Dome."

[22] McGrain, 273 U.S. at 321.

[23] Id. at 179-80.

[24] Id. at 177-78.

[25] Shelton v. United States, 404 F.2d 1292, 1297 (D.C. Cir. 1968), cert denied, 393 U.S. 1024 (1969).

[26] Barenblatt v. United States, 360 U.S. 109 (1959).

[27] Quinn v. United States, 349 U.S. 155, 161 (1955).

[28] McGrain, 273 U.S. at 295.

[29] United States v. Rumely, 345 U.S. 4, 43-45 (1953); see also Watkins v. United States, 354 U.S. 178, 200 n.3 (1957).

[30] See, e.g., Barenblatt, 360 U.S. 109 (1959); Watkins, 354 U.S. 178 (1957); McPhaul v. United States, 364 U.S. 372 (1960).

[31] Hutcheson v. United States, 369 U.S. 599 (1962).

[32] Shelton v. United States, 404 F.2d 1292, 1292 (D.C. Cir. 1968).

[33] See United States v. Icardi, 140 F. Supp. 383 (D.D.C. 1956); United States v. Cross, 170 F. Supp. 303 (D.D.C. 1959).

[34] Watkins v. United States, 354 U.S. 178, 200 (1957). However, Chief Justice Warren, writing for the majority, made it clear that he was not referring to the "power of the Congress to inquire into and publicize corruption, maladministration or inefficiency in agencies of the Government." Id.

[35] Barenblatt, 360 U.S. at 132.

[36] Positions of the Exec. Dept. Regarding Investigative Reports, 40 Op. A.G. 45. 46-47 (1941).

[37] See Appendix section "Investigation of Withholding EPA Documents."

[38] Letter to Hon. John D. Dingell Chairman, House Subcommittee on Oversight and Investigation, Committee on Energy and Commerce, from Attorney General William French Smith, dated November 30, 1982, reprinted in H.Rept. No. 97-968 at 37-38 [hereinafter Dingell Letter].

[39] Id. (quoting former Deputy Assistant General Thomas E. Kauper).

[40] Id.

[41] See Appendix section "Misuse of Informants in the FBI's Boston Regional Office."

[42] Investigation Into Allegations of Justice Department Misconduct In New England-Volume I, Hearings Before the H. Comm. on Government Reform, 107th Cong. 520-56, 562-604 (May 3, December 13, 2001; Feb. 6, 2002).

[43] Letter from Attorney Gen. Eric Holder to President Obama (June 19, 2012) available at http://www.justice.gov/olc/ 2012/ag-ff-exec-priv.pdf [hereinafter June 19 Letter].

[44] See discussion of case law, supra at notes 7-35, and accompanying text.

[45] Hutcheson v. United States, 369 U.S. 599, 617 (1962).

[46] Id. at 617 n.16.

[47] Sinclair v. United States, 279 U.S. 263, 294 (1929).

[48] See, e.g., Delaney v. United States, 199 F.2d 107 (1st Cir. 1952); United States v. Mitchell, 372 F. Supp. 1259, 1261 (S.D.N.Y. 1973). For discussion of issues in addition to prejudicial publicity that have been raised in regard to concurrent congressional and judicial proceedings, including allegations of violation of due process, see, Contempt of Congress, H.R. REP. No. 97-968, at 58 (1982).

[49] 199 F.2d 107, 114 (1st Cir. 1952). The court did not fault the committee for holding public hearings, stating that if closed hearings were rejected "because the legislative committee deemed that an open hearing at that time was required by overriding considerations of public interest, then the committee was of course free to go ahead with its hearing, merely accepting the consequence that the trial of Delaney on the pending indictment might have to be delayed." Id. at 114-15. It reversed Delaney's conviction because the trial court had denied his motion for a continuance until after the publicity generated by the hearing, at which Delaney and other trial witnesses were asked to testify, subsided. See also Hutcheson, 369 U.S. at 613 (upholding contempt conviction of person who refused to answer committee questions relating to activities for which he had been indicted by a state grand jury, citing Delaney).

[50] 199 F.2d at 115.

[51] See Silverthorne v. United States, 400 F.2d 627 (9th Cir. 1968), cert. denied, 400 U.S. 102 (1971) (claim of prejudicial pretrial publicity rejected because committee hearings occurred

five months prior to indictment); Beck v. Washington, 369 U.S. 541, 544 (1962) (hearing occurred a year before trial); United States v. Haldeman, 559 F.2d 31, 63 (D.C. Cir. 1976), cert. denied, 433 U.S. 933 (1977); United States v. Ehrlichman, 546 F.2d 910, 917 (D.C. Cir. 1976), cert. denied, 429 U.S. 1120 (1977); United States v. Romano, 583 F. 2d. 1, 4 (1st Cir. 1978) (Senate Committee determined not to heed warnings from DOJ that insistence on defendant's testimony would threaten or absolutely bar future prosecutions but conviction was nonetheless upheld); United States v. Mitchell, 372 F. Supp. 1239, 1261 (S.D.N.Y. 1973) (post-indictment Senate hearing but court held that lapse of time and efforts of committee to avoid questions relating to indictment diminished possibility of prejudice); United States v. Mesarosh, 223 F.2d 449 (3rd Cir. 1955) (hearing only incidentally connected with trial and occurred after jury selected).

[52] See, e.g., Pillsbury Co. v. FTC, 354 F.2d 952 (5th Cir. 1968).

[53] See, e.g., ATX, Inc. v. Dep't of Transportation, 41 F.3d 1522 (D.C. Cir. 1994); State of California v. FERC, 966 F.2d 154 (9th Cir. 1992); Peter Kiewet Sons' v. U.S. Army Corps of Engineers, 714 F.2d 163 (D.C. Cir. 1983); Gulf Oil Corp. v. FPC, 563 F.2d 588 (3d Cir. 1977), cert. denied, 434 U.S. 1062 (1978); United States v. Armada Petroleum Corp., 562 F. Supp 43 (S.D. Tex. 1982). See also CRS Report RL32113, Congressional Intervention in the Administrative Process: Legal and Ethical Considerations, by Jack Maskell, September 25, 2003.

[54] Lawrence E. Walsh, The Independent Counsel and the Separation of Powers, 25 HOUS. L. REV. 1, 9 (1988).

[55] Response to Congressional Requests for Information Regarding Decisions Made Under the Independent Counsel Act, 10 Op. O.L.C. 68, 76 (1986).

[56] See Appendix section "Operation Fast and Furious."

[57] See, e.g., Neal Devins, Congressional-Executive Information Access Disputes: A Modest Proposal: Do Nothing, 48 ADMIN. L. REV. 109-137 (1996); Joel D. Bush, Congressional-Executive Access Disputes: Legal Standards and Political Settlements, 9 J.L. & POL. 717 (1993); Stephen W. Stathis, Executive Cooperation: Presidential Recognition of the Investigatory Authority of Congress and the Courts, 3 J.L. & POL. 183 (1986).

[58] See Appendix section "Operation Fast and Furious."

[59] In total, there have been four cases dealing with executive privilege in the context of information access disputes between Congress and the Executive, United States v. Am. Tel. & Tel. Co., 551 F.2d 384 (D.C. Cir. 1976); Senate Select Committee, 498 F.2d 725; Miers, 558 F. Supp. 2d 53; House of Representatives, 556 F. Supp. 150 (D.D.C. 1983). Two of those resulted in decisions on the merits, Senate Select Committee and Miers. No decision of the Supreme Court has yet resolved the question of whether there are any circumstances in which the executive branch can refuse to provide information sought by Congress on the basis of executive privilege.

[60] 567 F.2d 121 (D.C. Cir. 1977) [hereinafter AT&T II].

[61] 556 F. Supp. 150 (D.D.C. 1983).

[62] Id. at 151. See Appendix section "Investigation of Withholding EPA Documents."

[63] House of Representatives, 556 F. Supp. at 152-53.

[64] 558 F. Supp. 2d 53 (D.D.C. 2008).

[65] Id. at 105.

[66] 121 F.3d 729 (D.C. Cir. 1997).

[67] 365 F.3d 1108 (D.C. Cir. 2004). The panel split 2-1, with Judge Rogers writing for the majority and Judge Randolph dissenting.

68 See Nixon v. Sirica, 487 F.2d 750 (D.C. Cir. 1973); Senate Select Committee, 498 F.2d 725. United States v. Nixon, 418 U.S. 683 (1974) and Nixon v. Administrator of General Services, 433 U.S. 425 (1977) are the only executive privilege cases to be decided by the Supreme Court.

69 In re Sealed Case (Espy), 121 F.3d 729, 745-46 (D.C. Cir. 1997) [hereinafter Espy]; see also id. at 737-38 ("[W]here there is reason to believe the documents sought may shed light on government misconduct, the [deliberative process] privilege is routinely denied on the grounds that shielding internal government deliberations in this context does not serve 'the public interest in honest, effective government.'").

70 Id. at 745, 752; see also id. at 753 ("... these communications nonetheless are ultimately connected with presidential decisionmaking").

71 Id. at 754, 757.

72 The President has delegated the formal process of review and recommendation of his pardon authority to the Attorney General who, in turn, has delegated it to the Deputy Attorney General. The Deputy Attorney General oversees the work of the Office of the Pardon Attorney.

73 Judicial Watch v. Department of Justice, 365 F.3d 1108, 1109-12 (D.C. Cir. 2004).

74 Id. at 1112.

75 Id. at 1116-18.

76 Espy, 121 F.3d at 757.

77 Id. at 752.

78 487 U.S. 654 (1988).

79 Id. at 691-92.

80 Senate Select Committee, 498 F.2d at 731.

81 Espy, 121 F.3d at 745-46. See also id. at 737-38 ("[W]here there is reason to believe the documents sought may shed light on government misconduct, the [deliberative process] privilege is routinely denied on the grounds that shielding internal government deliberations in this context does not serve 'the public interest in honest, effective government.'").

82 International Uranium Cartel Vol. 1, H. Comm. on Interstate and Foreign Commerce, Subcomm. on Oversight and Investigations, 95th Cong. 123 (1977). See CRS Report 95-464, Investigative Oversight: An Introduction to the Law, Practice and Procedure of Congressional Inquiry, 43-55 (out of print; available from the authors); see also Glenn A. Beard, Congress v. the Attorney-Client Privilege: A "Full and Frank Discussion," 35 AMER. CRIM. L. REV. 119, 122-127 (1997) ("[C]ongressional witnesses are not legally entitled to the protection of the attorney-client privilege, and investigating committees therefore have discretionary authority to respect or overrule such claims as they see fit."); Thomas Millett, The Applicability of Evidentiary Privileges for Confidential Communications Before Congress, 21 JOHN MARSHALL L. REV. 309 (1988).

83 Eastland v. United States Servicemen's Fund, 421 U.S. 491, 504 n.15. (1975); Watkins v. United States, 354 U.S. 178, 187 (1957); McGrain v. Daugherty, 273 U.S. 135, 177 (1927).

84 Westinghouse Electric Corp. v. Republic of the Philippines, 951 F.2d 1414, 1423 (3d Cir. 1991).

85 Opinion No. 288, Compliance With Subpoena from Congressional Committee to Produce Lawyers' Files Containing Client Confidences or Secrets, Legal Ethics Committee, District of Columbia Bar, Feb. 16, 1999 (D.C Ethics Committee Opinion).

86 A direct suit to enjoin a committee from enforcing a subpoena has been foreclosed by the Supreme Court's decision in Eastland, 421 U.S. at 501, but that ruling does not appear to foreclose an action against a "third party," such as the client's attorney, to test the validity

of the subpoena or the power of a committee to refuse to recognize the privilege. See, e.g., AT&T II, 567 F. 2d 121 (entertaining an action by the Justice Department to enjoin AT&T from complying with a subpoena to provide telephone records that might compromise national security matters).

87 These sensitive materials included prosecutorial memoranda, FBI investigative reports, summaries of FBI interviews, memoranda and correspondence prepared during the pendency of cases, confidential instructions outlining the procedures or guidelines to be followed for undercover operations and the surveillance and arrest of subjects, and documents presented to grand juries not protected from disclosure by Rule 6(e) of the Federal Rules of Criminal Procedure. Additionally, investigating committees often obtained the testimony of subordinate DOJ employees, such as line attorneys and FBI field agents, both formally and informally, on specific matters of DOJ's operations.

88 Resignations have included Attorneys General Harry M. Daugherty (1924), J. Howard McGrath (1952), Alberto R. Gonzales (2007).

89 Attorneys General Richard Kleindienst was convicted of perjury (1973) and John Mitchell was convicted of obstruction of justice, conspiracy, and perjury (1975).

90 See Charges of Illegal Practices of the Department of Justice: Hearings Before a Subcomm. of the Senate Comm. on the Judiciary, 66th Cong. (1921) [hereinafter Senate Palmer Hearings]; Attorney General A. Mitchell Palmer on Charges Made Against Department of Justice by Louis F. Post and Others: Hearings Before the H. Comm. on Rules, 66th Cong. (1920) [hereinafter House Palmer Hearings].

91 Senate Palmer Hearings at 38-98, 421-86, 539-63; House Palmer Hearings at 3-209.

92 E.g., Senate Palmer Hearings at 431-43, 458-69, 472-76.

93 Id. at 12-14, 18-19.

94 Id. at 484-538. See also Harlan Grant Cohen, The (Un)Favorable Judgment of History: Deportation Hearings, the Palmer Raids, and the Meaning of History, 78 NYU L. REV. 1431, 1451-56 (2003) (recounting historical context of Palmer Raids).

95 McGrain v. Daugherty, 273 U.S. 135, 151 (1927).

96 Investigation of Hon. Harry M. Daugherty, Formerly Attorney General of the United States: Hearings Before the S. Select Comm. on Investigation of the Attorney General vols. 1-3, 68th Cong. (1924) [hereinafter Daugherty Hearings].

97 See id. at 1495-1503, 1529-30, 2295-96.

98 Id. at 1120.

99 Id. at 1078-79.

100 Id. at 1015-16, 1159-60.

101 Id. at 2389.

102 Id. at 1495-1547.

103 Daugherty Hearings at 1790.

104 McGrain, 273 U.S. 135.

105 Id. at 177.

106 279 U.S. 263 (1929).

107 Id. at 290.

108 Id. at 295.

109 Id.

110 Investigations of the Dep't of Justice: Hearings Before the Special Subcomm. to Investigate the Dep't of Justice of the H. Comm. on the Judiciary, pt 1 & 2, 82nd Cong. (1952), part 1 & 2, 83rd Cong. (1953) [hereinafter DOJ Investigation Hearings]. The subcommittee summarized its conclusions about its inquiries during the 82nd Congress in Investigation of

the Department of Justice, H.R. REP. No. 1079, 83rd Cong. (1953) [hereinafter DOJ Investigation Report].

[111] DOJ Investigation Hearings at 753.

[112] See id. at 1256-57, 1270-71.

[113] Id. at 759-66. Other memoranda and documents from the Department were reviewed by the Subcommittee and kept in its confidential files. For example, these documents included a letter of instruction from the Attorney General to the Department attorney that had been sent to St. Louis. Id. at 890. In addition, the district court judge that had convened the grand jury gave the subcommittee permission to use the notes of the U.S. Attorney in St. Louis and of one of the grand jurors, with all names deleted. Id. The judge also submitted a deposition to the subcommittee about the Department's interference with the grand jury. Id. at 891-93.

[114] Id. at 754.

[115] Id.

[116] Id. at 766-808.

[117] Id. at 808-94, 1064-1117, 1256-1318.

[118] DOJ Investigation Hearings at 811.

[119] Id. at 1653-1812.

[120] Id. at 1579-80.

[121] DOJ Investigation Report at 69.

[122] Id.

[123] DOJ Investigation Hearings at 895-964.

[124] Id. at 897.

[125] DOJ Investigation Hearings at 26.

[126] Id.

[127] Id. at 25-294.

[128] Id. at 62-63, 233-34, 239-41, 258-59, 262, 269-73.

[129] See Consent Degree Program of the Department of Justice: Hearings before the Antitrust Subcomm. (Subcomm. No. 5) of the H. Comm. on the Judiciary, pt. 1-2, 85th Cong. (1957-58) [hereinafter Consent Decree Hearings]; REPORT OF THE ANTITRUST SUBCOMM. (SUBCOMM. NO. 5), OF THE H. COMM. ON THE JUDICIARY, 86TH CONG., REPORT ON CONSENT DECREE PROGRAM OF THE DEPT. OF JUSTICE (Comm. Print 1959) [hereinafter Consent Decree Report].

[130] Consent Decree Report at xiii.

[131] Consent Decree Hearings at 1674.

[132] Id. at 1674-75.

[133] Id. at 3706.

[134] Id. at 1675.

[135] Id.

[136] Consent Decree Report at 42.

[137] Id.

[138] Id.

[139] Consent Decree Hearings at 3647.

[140] Id. at 3711-44.

[141] See S. REP. NO. 755, Books 1-3, 94th Cong. (1976) [hereinafter Senate Intelligence Report]; Intelligence Activities, Senate Resolution 21: Hearings Before the Senate Select Comm. to Study Governmental Operations with Respect to Intelligence Activities, vols. 1-6, 94th Cong. (1975) [hereinafter Senate Intelligence Hearings]; FBI Oversight: Hearings Before

the Subcomm. on Civil and Constitutional Rights of the H. Comm. of the Judiciary, pt. 1-3, 94th Cong. (1975- 1976), pt. 1-2, 95th Cong. (1978) [hereinafter FBI Oversight Hearings].

[142] Senate Intelligence Report, Book 2, at ix n.7.

[143] Id.

[144] Senate Intelligence Hearings at iv n.1.

[145] Senate Intelligence Report, Book 2, ix n. 7.

[146] FBI Oversight Hearings pt. 2 at 1-2.

[147] Id. at 3. The review was ultimately reduced to 797 cases.

[148] Id. at 3-4.

[149] FBI Oversight Hearings pt. 1 at 103.

[150] See White Collar Crime in the Oil Industry: Joint Hearings before the Subcomm. on Energy and Power of the H. Comm. on Interstate and Foreign Commerce and the Subcomm. on Crime of the H. Comm. on the Judiciary, 96th Cong. (1979) [hereinafter White Collar Crime Hearings].

[151] White Collar Crime Hearings at 2.

[152] Id. at 134.

[153] Id. at 156-57.

[154] See Inquiry into the Matter of Billy Carter and Libya: Hearings Before the Subcomm. to Investigate the Activities of Individuals Representing the Interests of Foreign Governments of the Senate Comm. on the Judiciary, vols. 1-3, 96th Cong. (1980) [hereinafter Billy Carter Hearings]; Inquiry into the Matter of Billy Carter and Libya, S. REP. NO. 96- 1015 (1980) [hereinafter Billy Carter Report].

[155] Billy Carter Hearings at 116-30, 683-1153.

[156] Id. at 1741-42.

[157] Id. at 755-978.

[158] See Law Enforcement Undercover Activities: Hearings Before the Senate Select Comm. to Study Law Enforcement Undercover Activities of Components of the Department of Justice, 97th Cong. (1982) [hereinafter Abscam Hearings]; Final Report of the Senate Select Comm. to Study Undercover Activities of Components of the Department of Justice, S. REP. NO. 97-682 (1982) [hereinafter Abscam Report].

[159] Abscam Hearings at 10-85, 153-226, 255-559, 895-924, 1031-70.

[160] Abscam Report at 8-10.

[161] Id. at 486.

[162] Id.

[163] Id. at v.

[164] Id. at 9.

[165] Federal Rule of Criminal Procedure 6(e) bars disclosure of a "matter occurring before the grand jury" except, inter alia, by court order. FED. R. CRIM. P. 6(e).

[166] See generally Abscam Report at v, 472-84.

[167] Id. at v.

[168] Abscam Hearings at 514.

[169] Abscam Report at 485.

[170] Id. at 494.

[171] Id. at 498.

[172] Id. at 501.

[173] Id. at v.

[174] See FBI Undercover Activities, Authorization; and H.R. 3232: Oversight Hearings Before the Subcomm. on Civil and Constitutional Rights of the H. Comm. on the Judiciary, 98th Cong.

(1983); FBI Undercover Operations: Hearings Before the Subcomm. on Civil and Constitutional Rights of the H. Comm. on the Judiciary, 97th Cong. (1981); FBI Oversight: Hearings Before the Subcomm. on Civil and Constitutional Rights of the H. Comm. on the Judiciary, 96th Cong. (1979-80).

175 REPORT OF THE SUBCOMM. ON CIVIL AND CONST. RIGHTS OF THE H. COMM. ON THE JUDICIARY, FBI UNDERCOVER OPERATIONS, 98th Cong. 91-93 (Comm. Print 1984).

176 See H. REP. No. 97-968 (1982) [hereinafter Gorsuch Burford House Contempt Report].

177 Id. at 13-20.

178 See 8 Op. O.L.C. 101, 107 (1984) [hereinafter 1984 OLC Opinion].

179 See HoUse of Representatives, 556 F. Supp. 150; see also 2 U.S.C. §§192, 194.

180 See Memorandum of Understanding Between the Committee on Public Works and Transportation and the Department of Justice, Concerning Documents Subpoenaed from the Environmental Protection Agency, February 18, 1983; see also H. REP. No. 98-323, at 18-20 (1983).

181 See EPA Document Agreement, CQ WEEKLY REPORT, March 26, 1983 at 685.

182 Id.

183 Id.

184 Id.

185 See generally House of Representatives, 556 F. Supp. 150.

186 See Report of the House Comm. on the Judiciary on Investigation of the Role of the Department of Justice in the Withholding of Environmental Protection Agency Documents from Congress in 1982-1983, H. REP. 99-435 (1985) [hereinafter EPA Withholding Report].

187 EPA Withholding Report at 1163; see also id. at 1234-38.

188 Id. at 1164.

189 Id. at 1164-65, 1191-1231.

190 Id. at 1167, 1182-83.

191 Id. at 1184.

192 Id. at 1168, 1233.

193 EPA Withholding Report at 1168.

194 Id. at 1169.

195 Id. at 1172.

196 Id. at 1173.

197 Id. at 1174-76.

198 Id. at 1176-77, 1263-64.

199 EPA Withholding Report at 1265.

200 Id.

201 Id. at 1266.

202 Id.

203 Id. at 1268-69.

204 Id. at 1269-70.

205 EPA Withholding Report at 1270.

206 See E.F. HUTTON MAIL AND WIRE FRAUD, REPORT OF THE H. SUBCOMM. ON CRIME, H. COMM. ON THE JUDICIARY, 99th Cong. (Comm. Print, Serial No. 13, December 1986) [hereinafter Hutton Report].

207 Hutton Report at 1119.

[208] 610 F.2d 202, 216-17 (5th Cir. 1982) (opinions or statement based on knowledge of grand jury proceedings may be disclosed "provided, of course, the statement does not reveal the grand jury information on which it is based").

[209] Hutton Report at 1217.

[210] Id. at 1218. See FED. R. CRIM. P. 6(e).

[211] Hutton Report at 1328.

[212] See id. at 1329-35.

[213] See Report of the Congressional Committees Investigating the Iran-Contra Affair, H. REP. No. 433 & S. REP. No. 216, 100th Cong. 310, 317, 314, 317-18, 647 (1987).

[214] See Environmental Crimes at the Rocky Flats Nuclear Weapons Facility: Hearings Before the Subcomm. on Investigations and Oversight of the H. Comm. on Science, Space and Technology, vols. I and II, 102nd Cong. (1992) [hereinafter Rocky Flats Hearings]; Meetings: To Subpoena Appearance by Employees of the Department of Justice and the FBI and To Subpoena Production of Documents From Rockwell International Corporation, Meetings Before the Subcomm. on Investigations and Oversight of the H. Comm. on Science, Space, and Technology, 102nd Cong. No. 146 (1992) [hereinafter Subpoena Meetings].

[215] Rocky Flats Hearing, vol. I, at 389-1009, 1111-1251.

[216] Id. at 9-10, 25-31, 1673-1737; Subpoena Hearings at 1-3, 82-86, 143-51.

[217] See DAMAGING DISARRAY: ORGANIZATIONAL BREAKDOWN AND REFORM IN THE JUSTICE DEPARTMENT'S ENVIRONMENTAL CRIMES PROGRAM, A STAFF REPORT PREPARED FOR THE USE OF THE SUBCOMM. ON OVERSIGHT AND INVESTIGATIONS OF THE H. COMM. ON ENERGY AND COMMERCE, 103rd Cong. 1-4, 10-40 (Comm. Print 1994).

[218] The Federal Raid on Ruby Ridge, Idaho: Hearings before the Senate Subcommittee on Terrorism, Technology, Government Information, Committee on the Judiciary, 104th Cong. (1995) [hereinafter Ruby Ridge Hearings].

[219] Ruby Ridge: Report of the Subcommittee on Terrorism, Technology and Government Information of the Senate Committee on the Judiciary [hereinafter Ruby Ridge Report]. The 154-page document appears not to have been officially reported by the full Committee. A bound copy may be found in the United States Senate Library, catalogue number HV 8141.U56 1995.

[220] Ruby Ridge Report at 1; Ruby Ridge Hearings at 722, 954, 961.

[221] See generally Ruby Ridge Report.

[222] Weaver was convicted for failure to appear for a trial and for commission of an offense while on release.

[223] See, e.g., Ruby Ridge Hearings at 719-37, 941-85; Ruby Ridge Report at 10-11 ("With the exceptions of the [Ruby Ridge] Task Force Report, which was partially disavowed by the Department, and the April 5, 1995 memorandum of Deputy Attorney General Jamie Gorelick, it appeared to the subcommittee that the authors of every report we read were looking more to justify agency conduct than to follow the facts wherever they lead."); see also id. at 61-69, 115, 122- 23, 134-35, 139, 145-49; David Johnston, Idaho Siege Report Says F.B.I. Agents Violated Procedure, N.Y. TIMES, December 13, 1994, at A1.

[224] See The Justice Department's Handling of the Yah Lin "Charlie" Trie Case: Hearing before the Senate Comm. on Governmental Affairs, 106th Cong. 3-4, 14-63, 105-33 (1999).

[225] See, e.g., Roberto Suro, FBI to Brief 2 Lawmakers on Details of Freeh's Memo; Document on Independent Counsel Recommendation Won't Be Shared in Fund-Raising Probe, WASH. POST, December 18, 1997, at A04; Robert Suro, Freeh's Tightrope Act Plays Well on the

Hill; FBI Chief Retains Equilibrium, Displays Political Skill Despite Pressure From Many Sides, WASH. POST, December 11, 1997, at A14; Editorial Desk, Mr. Freeh's Truth Grenade, N.Y. TIMES, December 3, 1997, at A34; Francis X. Clines, The Attorney General's Decision: The Dissenter; Rebuffed, FBI Chief Skips Reno's Statement on Counsel, N.Y. TIMES, December 3, 1997, at A30.

[226] See Contempt of Congress, Report of the Comm. on Government Reform and Oversight on the Refusal of Attorney General Janet Reno to Produce Documents Subpoenaed by the Government Reform and Oversight Comm., H.Rept. 105-728 (1998).

[227] Justice Department's Implementation of the Independent Counsel Act, Hearing before the H. Comm. on Government Reform, 106th Cong., No. 106-231, June 6, 2000, at 5 [hereinafter Independent Counsel Hearing]; see, e.g., George Stuteville, Burton's Inquiry Puts Heat on Gore; Justice Memos on Alleged Fund-Raising Abuses Driving Probe, Congressman Says, THE INDIANAPOLIS STAR, June 18, 2000, at 01A.

[228] See Independent Counsel Hearing at 5.

[229] See id. See, e.g., Evidence Ignored in Funds Probe? Report Urged Look at Clinton, Gore, THE ATLANTA JOURNAL AND CONSTITUTION, June 8, 2000, at 12A; David Johnston, Papers Reveal Bitter Battle over Fund-Raising Inquiry, N.Y. TIMES, June 7, 2000, A26.

[230] Everything Secret Degenerates: The FBI's Use of Murderers As Informants, H.Rept. 108-414, 129 (2004) [hereinafter Everything Secret].

[231] Id. at 130.

[232] Id. at 2-9.

[233] Memorandum for the Attorney General from President George W. Bush, Congressional Subpoena for Executive Branch Documents, December 12, 2001, available at http://www.gpo.gov/fdsys/pkg/WCPD-2001-12-17/html/WCPD2001-12-17-Pg1783.htm.

[234] Id.

[235] See LOUIS FISHER, THE POLITICS OF EXECUTIVE PRIVILEGE, 108 (2004) [hereinafter FISHER].

[236] Letter from Alberto R. Gonzales, Counsel to the President, to Rep. Dan Burton, chairman of H. Government Reform Comm., Jan. 10, 2002, at 1.

[237] See FISHER, supra note 238.

[238] Everything Secret at 2-9, 121-134; Investigation Into Allegations of Justice Department Misconduct In New England-Volume I, Hearings Before the H. Comm. on Government Reform, 107th Cong. 520-556, 562-604 (May 3, December 13, 2001; Feb. 6, 2002). See, e.g., McIntyre v. United States, 367 F.3d 38, 42-51 (1st Cir. 2004) (recounting background of FBI corrupt activities); United States v. Salemme, 91 F. Supp. 2d 141, 148-63, 208-15, 322 (D. Mass. 1993); United States v. Flemmi, 195 F. Supp. 2d 243, 249-50 (D. Mass. 2001); Charles Tiefer, President Bush's First Executive Privilege Claim: The FBI/Boston Investigation, 33 PRES. STUD. Q. 201 (2003).

[239] Shelly Murphy & Brian R. Ballou, FBI Condemned in Landmark Ruling, BOSTON GLOBE, July 27, 2007, at A3; Robert Barrens & Paul Lewis, FBI Must Pay $102 Million In Mob Case, WASH. POST, July 27, 2007, at A3.

[240] See Everything Secret at 3, 134-135.

[241] Restoring Checks and Balances in the Confirmation Process of United States Attorneys, Hearing Before the Subcomm. on Commercial and Administrative Law, H. Committee on the Judiciary, 110th Cong., March 6, 2007; Ensuring Executive Branch Accountability, Hearing Before the Subcomm. on Commercial and Administrative Law, H. Comm. on the Judiciary, 110th Cong., March 29, 2007; Continuing Investigation into the U.S. Attorneys

Controversy, Hearing Before the Subcomm. on Commercial and Administrative Law, H. Comm. on the Judiciary, 110th Cong., May 3, 2007; Continuing Investigation into the U.S. Attorneys Controversy and Related Matters (Part II), Hearing Before the Subcomm. on Commercial and Administrative Law, H. Comm. on the Judiciary, 110th Cong., June 21, 2007; Continuing Investigation into the U.S. Attorneys Controversy and Related Matters (Part III), Hearing Before the Subcomm. on Commercial and Administrative Law, H. Comm. on the Judiciary, 110th Cong., July 12, 2007.

[242] United States Department of Justice, Hearing Before the H. Comm. on the Judiciary, 110th Cong., May 10, 2007; Continuing Investigation into the U.S. Attorneys Controversy and Related Matters (Part I), Hearing Before the H. Comm. on the Judiciary, 110th Cong., May 23, 2007.

[243] Letter from Fred F. Fielding, Counsel to the President, to Chairman Leahy and Chairman Conyers, June 28, 2007, available at http://www.judiciary.senate.gov/resources/documents/upload/110thCongress-2007Documents.pdf at 108-111.

[244] Meeting to Consider: a Resolution and Report Recommending to the House of Representatives that Former White House Counsel Harriet Miers and White House Chief of Staff Joshua Bolten be Cited for Contempt of Congress, Committee on the Judiciary, U.S. House of Representatives, July 25, 2007, records available at http://judiciary.house.gov/hearings/July2007/hear_072507.html.

[245] Roll call vote available at http://www.cq.com/doc/floorvote-208660000.

[246] Letter from Michael B. Mukasey, Attorney General, to Speaker Nancy Pelosi, Feb. 29, 2008, available at http://legaltimes.typepad.com/files/mukasey_letter.pdf.

[247] Miers, 558 F. Supp. 2d at 98.

[248] Id. at 106.

[249] Id. at 108. See H.Rept. 110-423 (2007).

[250] Opening Statement of Henry A. Waxman, chairman, House Committee on Oversight and Government Reform, Hearing on White House Procedures for Safeguarding Classified Information, 110th Cong. H. REP. No. 110-28 (March 16, 2007).

[251] Letter from Henry A. Waxman, chairman, to Special Counsel Patrick J. Fitzgerald (July 16, 2007) available at http://oversight-archive.waxman.house.gov/documents/200812 05114 732. pdf.

[252] Draft Report of the H. Committee on Oversight and Government Reform Regarding President Bush's assertion of Executive Privilege in Response to the Committee Subpoena to Attorney General Michael B. Mukasey [hereinafter Draft Report] available at http://oversight-archive.waxman.house.gov/documents/20081205114333.pdf.

[253] Id.

[254] Id. On June 5, 2008, Chairman of the House Judiciary Committee John Conyers issued a request for, inter alia, interview reports with the Vice President from Mr. Fitzgerald's investigation. The Judiciary Committee issued a subpoena on June 27, 2008, to compel production of documents on a wide variety of matters, including the interview with the Vice President. On September 10, 2008, Conyers agreed to defer a scheduled vote on a contempt citation for Attorney General Mukasey after the Justice Department's Civil Rights Division complied with an unrelated request in the same subpoena – releasing 681 pages of materials related to a Georgia voter identification law.

[255] Letter from Keith B. Nelson, Principal Deputy Assistant Attorney General, to Henry A. Waxman, chairman (June 24, 2008) available at http://oversight-archive.waxman.house.gov/documents/20081205114732.pdf.

[256] Id.

[257] Id.

[258] Id.

[259] Letter from Henry A. Waxman, chairman, to Michael B. Mukasey, Attorney General (July 8, 2008) (quoting Closing Argument for the Prosecution (Feb. 20, 2007), United States v. Libby, 495 F. Supp. 2d 49 (D.D.C. 2007)) available at http://oversight-archive.waxman.house.gov/documents/20081205114732.pdf.

[260] Id. (citing Espy, 121 F.3d at 741).

[261] Id.

[262] Letter from Keith B. Nelson, Principal Deputy Attorney General, to Henry A. Waxman, chairman (July 16, 2008) available at http://oversight-archive.waxman.house.gov /documents/20081205114732.pdf.

[263] Letter from Michael B. Mukasey, Attorney General, to President George W. Bush (July 15, 2008) available at http://oversight-archive.waxman.house.gov/documents/ 20081205114732.pdf.

[264] Id.

[265] Id. (quoting Senate Select Committee, 498 F.2d at 733 (holding that "the need demonstrated by the Select Committee ... is too attenuated and too tangential to its functions to permit a judicial judgment that the President is required to comply with the Committee's subpoena for production of tape recordings" between the President and his aide)).

[266] Id.

[267] Draft Report at 6.

[268] Citizens for Responsibility & Ethics in Washington v. U.S. Dept. of Justice, 658 F. Supp. 2d 217, 220, 226 (D.D.C. 2009).

[269] For a detailed discussion of Operation Fast and Furious, see CRS Report RL32842, Gun Control Legislation, by William J. Krouse. The Senate and House Judiciary Committees also initiated contemporaneous investigations.

[270] James V. Grimaldi and Sari Horwitz, ATF Probe Strategy is Questioned, WASH. POST, February 2, 2011, at A4.

[271] Id.

[272] John Solomon, David Heath, and Gordon Witkin, "ATF Let Hundreds of U.S. Weapons Fall into Hands of Suspected Mexican Gun Runners: Whistleblower Says Agents Strongly Objected to Risky Strategy," Center for Public Integrity, available at http://www.iwatchnews.org/2011/03/03/2095/atf-let-hundreds-us-weapons-fall-hands-suspected-mexican-gunrunners.

[273] Letter from Senator Charles Grassley to Acting Director of ATF Kenneth E. Melson (January 27, 2011) available at http://www.grassley.senate.gov/about/upload/Judiciary-01-27-11-letter-to-ATF-SW-Border-strategy.pdf.

[274] Letter from Ass't Att'y Gen. Ronald Weich to Senator Charles E. Grassley (February 4, 2011) available at http://www.grassley.senate.gov/about/upload/Judiciary-ATF-02-04-11-letter-from-DOJ-deny-allegations.pdf.

[275] Letter from Ass't Att'y Gen. Ronald Weich to Chairman Darrell Issa (June 14, 2011) (see Report of the Committee on Oversight and Government Reform, Resolution Recommending that the House of Representatives Find Eric H. Holder, Jr., Att'y Gen., U.S. Department of Justice, in Contempt of Congress for Refusal to Comply with a Subpoena Duly Issued by the Comm. on Oversight and Govt. Reform available at http://oversight.house.gov/wp-content/uploads/ 2012/06/Contempt-Report-final.pdf [hereinafter Holder Contempt Report]).

[276] Letter from Ass't Att'y Gen. Ronald Weich to Chairman Darrell Issa (October 11, 2011).

[277] Letter from Dep Att'y Gen. James M. Cole to Chairman Darrell Issa (December 2, 2011) available at http://www.scribd.com/doc/74797496/120211-Letter-to-Hon-Darrell-Issa-and-Hon-Charles-Grassley.

[278] Id.

[279] Id.

[280] Letter from Dep Att'y Gen. James M. Cole to Chairman Darrell Issa et al., (Jan. 27, 2012).

[281] Letter from Dep Att'y Gen. James M. Cole to Chairman Darrell Issa (Feb. 1, 2012).

[282] Letter from Chairman Issa to Att'y Gen. Eric Holder (Jan. 31, 2012) available at http://oversight.house.gov/wpcontent/uploads/2012/03/2012-01-31_DEI_to_Holder_re_Feb_4_deadline.pdf.

[283] See Holder Contempt Report, supra note 278.

[284] Id.

[285] Letter from Dep Att'y Gen. James M. Cole to Chairman Darrell Issa (May 15, 2012) available at http://online.wsj.com/public/resources/documents/DAGLetter5-15-12.pdf.

[286] Id. (quoting Prosecution for Contempt of Congress of an Executive Branch Official Who Has Asserted a Claim of Executive Privilege, Theodore B. Olson, Ass't Att'y Gen., 8 Op. O.L.C. 101 (May 30, 1984)).

[287] Id. (quoting Congressional Requests for Information from Inspectors General Concerning Open Criminal Investigations, Douglas W. Kmiec, Ass't Att'y Gen., 13 Op. O.L.C. 93 (March 24, 1989)).

[288] Id. (quoting Position of the Executive Department Regarding Investigative Reports, Robert Jackson, Attorney General, 40 Op. Att'y Gen. 45, 46 (1941)).

[289] Id. (pointing to Assertion of Executive Privilege Regarding White House Counsel's Office Documents, Janet Reno, Att'y Gen., 20 Op. O.L.C. 2, 3 (1996)).

[290] Letter from Chairman Issa to Att'y Gen. Eric Holder (June 13, 2012) available at http://oversight.house.gov/wpcontent/uploads/2012/06/2012-06-13-DEI-to-Holder-DOJ-contempt-settlement-letter.pdf.

[291] Holder Contempt Report, supra note 278, at 41-42.

[292] June 19 Letter, supra note 43.

[293] Id. Citing for support Letter for the President from Paul D. Clement, Solicitor Gen. and Acting Att'y Gen., Re: Assertion of Executive Privilege Concerning the Dismissal and Replacement of U.S. Attorneys (June 27, 2007) [hereinafter US Attorneys]; Assertion of Executive Privilege Regarding White House Counsel's Office Documents, 20 Op. O.L.C. 2, 3 (1996) [hereinafter WHCO]; Letter for the President from Michael B. Mukasey, Att'y Gen., Re: Assertion of Executive Privilege Concerning the Special Counsel's Interviews of the Vice President and Senior White House Staff (July 15, 2008) [hereinafter Special Counsel].

[294] June 19 Letter, supra note 43, at 3 (quoting WHCO, supra note 296, 20 Op. O.L.C. at 3).

[295] June 19 Letter, supra note 43, at 3 (quoting US Attorneys, supra note 296, at 6).

[296] Id. (quoting Letter for John Conyers, Jr., chairman, Comm. on the Judiciary, and Linda T. Sanchez, Chairwoman, Subcomm. on Commercial and Administrative Law, Committee on the Judiciary, U.S. House of Representatives, from Richard A. Bertling, Acting Assistant Attorney General, Office of Legislative Affairs at 3 (Mar. 26, 2007)).

[297] Id. (quoting Senate Select Committee, 498 F.2d at 731).

[298] Id. (quoting Special Counsel and referencing McGrain v. Daugherty, 273 U.S. 135, 176 (1927) and Eastland v U.S. Servicemen's Fund, 421 U.S. 491, 504 n.15 (1975) for support).

[299] June 19 Letter, supra note 43, at 6.

[300] Id. at 7.

[301] Id. (quoting Miller v. Transamerican Press, Inc., 709 F.2d 524, 531 (9th Cir. 1983)).
[302] Emphasis in letter.
[303] See H.Res. 711 (roll call vote available at http://cq.com/doc/floorvote-236138000).
[304] H.Res. 706, 112th Cong. (2012).
[305] Id. (roll call vote available at http://cq.com/doc/floorvote-236141000).
[306] See supra Appendix sections "Burford I: The Superfund Investigation" and "Removal and Replacement of United States Attorneys."
[307] Letter from James M. Cole, Deputy Attorney General, to John Boehner, Speaker of the House, June 28, 2012.
[308] Federal courts have generally adopted a deferential view of whether a congressional committee was pursuing a valid legislative purpose. See, "Legislative Purpose" infra.
[309] For a detailed discussion of executive privilege see, CRS Report RL30319, Presidential Claims of Executive Privilege: History, Law, Practice, and Recent Developments, by Todd Garvey and Alissa M. Dolan (out of print; available from the authors).
[310] Complaint, Committee on Oversight and Government Reform v. Holder, No. 1:12-cv-1332 (D.D.C. August 13, 2012).

In: Congressional Investigations …
Editor: Nathan De Vos

ISBN: 978-1-62808-073-5

Chapter 2

PRESIDENTIAL CLAIMS OF EXECUTIVE PRIVILEGE: HISTORY, LAW, PRACTICE, AND RECENT DEVELOPMENTS*

Todd Garvey and Alissa M. Dolan

SUMMARY

Presidential claims of a right to preserve the confidentiality of information and documents in the face of legislative demands have figured prominently, though intermittently, in executive-congressional relations since at least 1792. Few such interbranch disputes over access to information have reached the courts for substantive resolution. The vast majority of these disputes are resolved through political negotiation and accommodation. In fact, it was not until the Watergate-related lawsuits in the 1970's seeking access to President Nixon's tapes that the existence of a presidential confidentiality privilege was judicially established as a necessary derivative of the President's status in our constitutional scheme of separated powers. There have been only four cases involving information access disputes between Congress and the executive, and two of these resulted in decisions on the merits. The Nixon and post-Watergate cases established the broad contours of the presidential communications privilege. Under those precedents, the privilege, which

* This is an edited, reformatted and augmented version of a Congressional Research Service publication, CRS Report for Congress R42670, from www.crs.gov, prepared for Members and Committees of Congress, dated August 21, 2012.

is constitutionally rooted, could be invoked by the President when asked to produce documents or other materials or information that reflect presidential decision making and deliberations that he believes should remain confidential.

If the President asserts the privilege, the materials become presumptively privileged. The privilege, however, is qualified, not absolute, and can be overcome by an adequate showing of need. Finally, while reviewing courts have expressed reluctance in balancing executive privilege claims against a congressional demand for information, they have acknowledged they will do so if the political branches have tried, in good faith, but failed to reach an accommodation.

Until the District of Columbia Circuit's 1997 ruling in In re Sealed Case (Espy), and its 2004 decision in Judicial Watch v. Department of Justice, these earlier judicial decisions left considerable gaps in the law of presidential privilege.

Among the more significant issues left open included whether the President has to have actually seen or been familiar with the disputed matter; whether the presidential privilege encompasses documents and information developed by, or in the possession of, officers and employees in the departments and agencies of the Executive Branch, outside of the Executive Office of the President; whether the privilege encompasses all communications with respect to which the President may be interested or is confined to presidential decision making and, if so, is limited to a particular type of presidential decision making; and precisely what kind of demonstration of need must be shown to overcome the privilege and compel disclosure of the materials. The unanimous panel in Espy, and the subsequent reaffirmation of the Espy principles articulated in Judicial Watch, addressed each of these issues in a manner that may have drastically altered the future legal playing field in resolving such disputes. A more recent dispute with Congress involving the removal and replacement of nine United States Attorneys drew formal claims of privilege by President George W. Bush. Those privilege claims were challenged in a civil suit brought by the House Judiciary Committee seeking declaratory and injunctive relief with respect to refusals to appear, to testify, and to provide documents by two subpoenaed present and former officials. A district court decision on the merits, upholding the committee's challenge supplements the D.C. Circuit case law on this issue.

President Obama formally invoked executive privilege for the first time on June 20, 2012, over documents sought by the House Committee on Oversight and Government Reform in its ongoing investigation into Operation Fast and Furious.

INTRODUCTION

Presidential claims of a right to preserve the confidentiality of information and documents in the face of legislative demands have figured prominently, though intermittently, in executive-congressional relations since at least 1792, when President Washington discussed with his cabinet how to respond to a congressional inquiry into the military debacle that befell General St. Clair's expedition.[1] Few such interbranch disputes over access to information have reached the courts for substantive resolution; the vast majority achieve resolution through political negotiation and accommodation.[2] In fact, it was not until the Watergate-related lawsuits in the 1970's seeking access to President Nixon's tapes that the existence of a presidential confidentiality privilege was judicially established as a necessary derivative of the President's status in the U.S. constitutional scheme of separated powers. Litigation over the scope of executive privilege in direct relation to congressional oversight and investigations has also been quite limited. In total, there have been only four cases dealing with executive privilege in the context of information access disputes between Congress and the Executive,[3] and only two of those resulted in decisions on the merits.[4] Indeed, the Supreme Court has never addressed executive privilege in the face of a congressional demand for information.

The Nixon era cases initially established the broad contours of the presidential communications privilege. Under those precedents, the privilege, which is constitutionally rooted, could be invoked by the President when asked to produce documents or other materials or information that reflect presidential decision making and deliberations that he believes should remain confidential. If the President does so, the materials become presumptively privileged. The privilege, however, is qualified, not absolute, and can be overcome by an adequate showing of need. Finally, while reviewing courts have expressed reluctance in balancing executive privilege claims against a congressional demand for information, they have acknowledged they will do so if the political branches have tried in good faith but failed to reach an accommodation.

However, until the District of Columbia Circuit's 1997 ruling in *In re Sealed Case* (*Espy*)[5] and its 2004 decision in *Judicial Watch v. Department of Justice*,[6] existing precedent left important gaps in the law of presidential privilege that have increasingly become focal points, if not the source, of interbranch confrontations. Many significant issues remained unresolved, including whether the President has to have actually seen or been familiar with the disputed matter; whether the presidential privilege encompasses documents and information developed by, or in the possession of, officers and employees in the departments and agencies of the Executive Branch outside the Executive Office of the President; whether the privilege encompasses all communications in which the President may be interested or if it is confined to presidential decision making or a particular type of presidential decision making; and precisely what kind of demonstration of need can justify the release of privileged materials. The unanimous panel in *Espy*, and the subsequent reaffirmation of the *Espy* principles in *Judicial Watch*, addressed each of these issues in a manner that may have drastically altered the future legal playing field in resolving such disputes.[7]

A more recent dispute with Congress involving the removal and replacement of nine United States Attorneys drew formal claims of privilege by President George W. Bush. Those privilege claims were successfully challenged in a civil suit brought by the House Judiciary Committee seeking declaratory and injunctive relief arising from refusals by subpoenaed present and former senior presidential aides to appear, testify, or provide documents.[8] The district court held that senior presidential advisors do not enjoy absolute immunity from compelled testimony or production of documents pursuant to a congressional subpoena.[9] Before discussing *Espy* and *Judicial Watch* in detail, it is useful to review and understand the prior case law and how it has affected the positions of the disputants.

THE WATERGATE CASES

In interbranch information disputes since the early 1980's, executive statements and positions taken to justify assertions of executive privilege have frequently rested upon explanations of executive privilege offered by the courts. To better understand the executive's stance in this area, and the potential impact the *Espy* and *Judicial Watch* rulings may have on those positions, this report will chronologically examine the development of the judiciary's approach to executive privilege and describe how the executive has adapted the judicial explanations of the privilege to support its arguments.

In *Nixon v. Sirica*,[10] the first of the Watergate cases, the Court of Appeals for the District of Columbia Circuit rejected President Nixon's claim that he was absolutely immune from all compulsory process whenever he asserted a formal claim of executive privilege. The court held that while presidential conversations are "presumptively privileged,"[11] the presumption could be overcome by an appropriate showing of public need by the branch seeking access to the conversations. In *Sirica,* "a uniquely powerful," albeit undefined, showing was deemed to have been made by the Special Prosecutor, who argued that the tapes subpoenaed by the grand jury contained evidence vital to determining whether probable cause existed that those indicted had committed crimes.[12]

The D.C. Circuit next addressed the Senate Watergate Committee's effort to gain access to five presidential tapes in *Senate Select Committee on Presidential Campaign Activities v. Nixon*.[13] The appeals court initially determined that "[t]he staged decisional structure established in *Nixon v. Sirica*" was applicable "with at least equal force here."[14] Thus, in order to overcome the presumptive privilege and require the submission of materials for court review, a strong showing of need had to be established. The appeals court held that the Committee had not met its burden of showing that "the subpoenaed evidence is demonstrably critical to the responsible fulfillment of the Committee's function."[15] It elaborated that, in view of the initiation of impeachment proceedings by the House Judiciary Committee, the overlap of the investigative objectives of both committees, and the fact that the impeachment committee already had the tapes sought by the Senate Committee, "the Select Committee's immediate *oversight* need for the subpoenaed tapes is, from a congressional perspective, merely cumulative."[16] Nor did the court feel that the Committee had shown that the subpoenaed materials were "critical to the performance of [its] *legislative functions*."[17] The court could discern "no specific legislative decisions that cannot responsibly be made without access to materials uniquely contained in the tapes or without resolution of the ambiguities that the [presidentially released] transcripts may contain."[18] The court concluded that the subsequently initiated and nearly completed work of the House Judiciary Committee had in effect preempted the Senate Committee: "More importantly ... there is no indication that the findings of the House Committee on the Judiciary and, eventually the House of Representatives itself, are so likely to be inconclusive or long in coming that the Select Committee needs immediate access of its own."[19]

The D.C. Circuit's view in *Senate Select Committee*, that the Watergate Committee's oversight need for the requested materials was "merely cumulative" in light of the then concurrent impeachment inquiry, has been utilized by the executive as the basis for arguing that Congress's interest in executive information is less compelling when a committee's function is oversight than when it is considering specific legislative proposals.[20] This approach, however, arguably misreads the carefully circumscribed holding of the court, and would seem to construe too narrowly the scope of Congress's investigatory powers.

The *Senate Select Committee* court's opinion took great pains to underline the unique and limiting nature of the case's factual and historical context. Thus it emphasized the overriding nature of the "events that have occurred since this litigation was begun and, indeed, since the District Court issued its decision."[21] These facts included the commencement of impeachment proceedings by the House Judiciary Committee, a committee with an "express constitutional source" of investigative power, whose "investigative objectives substantially overlap" those of the Senate Committee; the House Committee's present possession of the very tapes sought by the Select Committee, making the Senate Committee's need for the tapes "from a congressional perspective, merely cumulative;" the lack of evidence indicating that Congress itself attached any particular value to "having the presidential conversations scrutinized by two committees simultaneously;" that the need to possess the tapes in order to make "legislative judgments has been substantially undermined by subsequent events," including the public release of the tape transcripts by the President; the transfer of four of five of the original tapes to the district court; and the lack of any "indication that the findings of the House Committee on the Judiciary and, eventually, the House of Representatives itself, are so likely to be inconclusive or long in coming that the Select Committee needs immediate access of its own."[22]

The appeals court concluded by reiterating the uniqueness of the case's facts and temporal circumstances:

> We conclude that the need demonstrated by the Select Committee in the peculiar circumstances of this case, including the subsequent and on-going investigation of the House Judiciary Committee, is too attenuated and too tangential to its functions to permit a judicial judgment that the President is required to comply with the Committee's subpoena.[23]

The executive's position arguably ignores the roots of Congress's broad investigatory powers, which reach back to the establishment of the Constitution and have been continually reaffirmed by the Supreme Court. As George Mason recognized at the Constitutional Convention, Members of Congress "are not only Legislators but they possess inquisitorial power. They must meet frequently to inspect the Conduct of the public offices."[24] Woodrow Wilson remarked:

> Quite as important as legislation is vigilant oversight of administration; and even more important than legislation is the instruction and guidance in political affairs which the people might receive from a body which kept all national concerns suffused in a broad daylight of discussion .... The informing functions of Congress should be preferred even to its legislative function. The argument is not only that a discussed and interrogated administration is the only pure and efficient administration, but, more than that, that the only really self-governing people is that people which discusses and interrogates its administration.[25]

The Supreme Court has cited Wilson favorably on this point.[26] Moreover, the Court has failed to make any distinction between Congress's right to executive branch information to use in support of its oversight function versus its responsibility to enact, amend, and repeal laws. In fact, the Court has recognized that Congress's investigatory power "comprehends probes into departments of the Federal Government to expose corruption, inefficiency or waste."[27] Thus, to read *Senate Select Committee* as downplaying the status of oversight arguably ignores the court's very specific reasons for not enforcing the committee's subpoena under the unique circumstance of that case and creates a distinction between oversight and legislating that has yet to be embraced by the courts. Moreover, the *Senate Select Committee* panel's "demonstrably critical" standard for overcoming a president's presumptive claim of privilege is not reflected in any of the subsequent Supreme Court or appellate court rulings establishing a balancing test for overcoming the qualified presidential privilege.

Two months after the ruling in *Senate Select Committee*, the Supreme Court issued its unanimous ruling in *United States v. Nixon* (*Nixon I*),[28] which involved a judicial trial subpoena issued to the President at the request of the Watergate Special Prosecutor requesting tape recordings and documents relating to the President's conversations with close aides and advisors. For the first time, the Court found a constitutional basis for the doctrine of executive privilege in "the supremacy of each branch within its own assigned area of constitutional duties" and in the separation of powers.[29] Although it considered a president's communications with his close advisors to be "presumptively privileged," the Court rejected the President's contention that the privilege was absolute and precluded judicial review whenever it is asserted.[30] The Court acknowledged the need for confidentiality of high-level communications in the exercise of Article II powers, but stated that "a confrontation with other values arises" when the privilege is asserted based on a broad, undifferentiated claim of public interest in the confidentiality of such communications.[31] It held that "absent a need to protect military, diplomatic, or sensitive national security secrets, we find it difficult to accept the argument that even the very important interest in confidentiality of presidential communications is significantly diminished by production of" materials that are essential to the enforcement of criminal statutes.[32]

After concluding that the claim of privilege was qualified, the Court moved on to resolving the "competing interests" at stake: the President's need for confidentiality versus the judiciary's need for evidence in a criminal proceeding. Evaluating these interests "in a manner that preserves the essential functions of each branch,"[33] the Court held that the judicial need for the tapes, as shown by a "demonstrated, specific need for evidence in a pending criminal trial," outweighed the President's "generalized interest in confidentiality...."[34] The Court was careful, however, to limit the scope of its decision, noting that "we are not here concerned with the balance between the President's generalized interest in confidentiality ... and congressional demands for information."[35]

In the last of the Nixon cases, *Nixon v. Administrator of General Services* (*Nixon II*),[36] the Supreme Court again balanced competing interests in President Nixon's White House records. The Presidential Recordings and Materials Preservation Act[37] granted custody of President Nixon's presidential records to the Administrator of the General Services Administration who would screen them for personal and private materials, to be returned to President Nixon, and preserve the rest for historical and governmental objectives. The Court rejected President Nixon's challenge to the act, which included an argument based on the "presidential privilege of confidentiality."[38] Although *Nixon II* did not involve an executive response to a congressional probe, several points emerge from the Court's discussion that bear upon Congress's interest in confidential executive branch information. First, the Court reiterated that the executive privilege it had announced in *Nixon I* was not absolute, but qualified.[39] Second, the Court stressed the narrow scope of that executive privilege. "In [*Nixon I*] the Court held that the privilege is limited to communications 'in performance of [a President's] responsibilities ... of his office' ... and made in the process of shaping policies and making decisions."[40] Third, the Court found that there was a "substantial public interest[]" in preserving these materials so that Congress, pursuant to its "broad investigative power," could examine them to understand the events that led to President Nixon's resignation "in order to gauge the necessity for remedial legislation."[41]

POST-WATERGATE CASES

Two post-Watergate cases, both involving congressional demands for access to executive information, demonstrate both the judiciary's reluctance to get involved in the essentially political confrontations such disputes represent and a willingness to intervene where the political process appears to be failing.

In *United States v. AT&T*,[42] the D.C. Circuit was unwilling to balance executive privilege claims against a congressional demand for information unless and until the political branches had tried in good faith but failed to reach an accommodation.[43] In that case, the Justice Department sought to enjoin AT&T's compliance with a subpoena issued by a House subcommittee. The subcommittee was seeking FBI letters sent to AT&T requesting its assistance with warrantless wiretaps on U.S. citizens allegedly conducted for national security purposes. The Justice Department argued that the executive branch was entitled to sole control over the information because of "its obligation to safeguard the national security."[44] The House of Representatives, as intervenor, argued that its rights to the information flowed from its constitutionally implied power to investigate whether there had been abuses of the wiretapping power. The House also argued that the court had no jurisdiction over the dispute because of the Speech or Debate Clause.

The court rejected the "conflicting claims of the [Executive and the Congress] to absolute authority."[45] With regard to the executive's claim, the court noted that there was no absolute claim of executive privilege in response to congressional requests even in the area of national security:

> The executive would have it that the Constitution confers on the executive absolute discretion in the area of national security. This does not stand up. While the Constitution assigns to the President a number of powers relating to national security, including the function of commander in chief and the power to make treaties and appoint Ambassadors, it confers upon Congress other powers equally inseparable from the national security, such as the powers to declare war, raise and support armed forces and, in the case of the Senate, consent to treaties and the appointment of ambassadors.[46]

Likewise, the court rejected the congressional claim that the Speech or Debate Clause was "intended to immunize congressional investigatory actions from judicial review. Congress' investigatory power is not, itself, absolute."[47]

According to the court, judicial intervention in executive privilege disputes between the political branches is improper unless the branches have made a good faith effort at compromise without result.[48] The court held that there is a constitutional duty for the executive and Congress to attempt to accommodate each other's needs:

> The framers, rather than attempting to define and allocate all governmental power in minute detail, relied, we believe, on the expectation that where conflicts in scope of authority arose between the coordinate branches, a spirit of dynamic compromise would promote resolution of the dispute in the manner most likely to result in efficient and effective functioning of our governmental system. Under this view, the coordinate branches do not exist in an exclusively adversary relationship to one another when a conflict in authority arises. Rather, each branch should take cognizance of an implicit constitutional mandate to seek optimal accommodation through a realistic evaluation of the needs of the conflicting branches in the particular fact situation.[49]

The court refused to resolve the dispute because the executive and Congress had not yet made that constitutionally mandated effort at accommodation. Instead, the court "encouraged negotiations in order to avoid the problems inherent in [the judiciary] formulating and applying standards for measuring the relative needs of the [executive and legislative branches]."[50] The court suggested, however, that it would resolve the dispute if the political branches failed to reach an accommodation.[51] The court-encouraged negotiations ultimately led to a compromise. Subcommittee staff were allowed to review unedited memoranda describing the warrantless wiretaps and report orally to subcommittee Members. The Justice Department, however, retained custody of the documents.[52]

The U.S. District Court for the District of Columbia displayed the same reluctance to intervene in an executive privilege dispute with Congress in *United States v. House of Representatives.*[53] There the court dismissed a suit brought by the Justice Department seeking a declaratory judgment that the Administrator of the Environmental Protection Agency (EPA), Anne Gorsuch Burford, "acted lawfully in refusing to release certain documents to a congressional subcommittee" at the direction of the President.[54] The

Administrator based her refusal upon President Reagan's invocation of executive privilege against a House committee probing the EPA's enforcement of hazardous waste laws. The court dismissed the case, without reaching the executive privilege claim, on the ground that judicial intervention in a dispute "concerning the respective powers of the Legislative and Executive Branches ... should be delayed until all possibilities for settlement have been exhausted ... Compromise and cooperation, rather than confrontation, should be the aim of the parties."[55] As the appeals court had done in *AT&T*, the district court in *United States v. House of Representatives* encouraged the political branches to settle their dispute rather than invite judicial intervention. The court would intervene and resolve the interbranch dispute only if the parties could not agree. Even then, the courts advised, "Judicial resolution of this constitutional claim ... will never become necessary unless Administrator Gorsuch [Burford] becomes a defendant in either a criminal contempt proceeding or other legal action taken by Congress."[56] Ultimately the branches did reach an agreement, and the court did not need to balance executive and congressional interests.[57]

EXECUTIVE BRANCH POSITIONS ON THE SCOPE OF EXECUTIVE PRIVILEGE

Unsurprisingly, the executive branch has developed an expansive view of executive privilege in relation to congressional investigations, taking maximum advantage of the vague and essentially undefined terrain within the judicially recognized contours of the privilege. Thus, executive branch statements have identified four areas that it believes are presumptively covered by executive privilege: foreign relations and military affairs, two separate topics that are sometimes lumped together as "state secrets;" law enforcement investigations; and confidential information that reveals the executive's "deliberative process" with respect to policymaking.[58] Typically, the executive has asserted executive privilege based upon a combination of deliberative process and one or more of the other categories. Consequently, much of the controversy surrounding invocation of executive privilege has centered on the scope of the deliberative process category. The executive has argued that at its core this category protects confidential predecisional deliberative material from disclosure.[59] Justifications for this exemption often draw upon the language in *Nixon I* that identifies a constitutional value in the President receiving candid advice from his subordinates and awareness that any expectation of subsequent disclosure might temper needed candor.[60] The result has been a presumption by the executive that its predecisional deliberations are beyond the scope of congressional demand. "Congress will have a legitimate need to know the preliminary positions taken by Executive Branch officials during internal deliberations only in the rarest of circumstances."[61] According to this view, the need for the executive to prevent disclosure of its deliberations is at its apex when Congress attempts to discover information about ongoing policymaking within the executive branch. In that case, the executive has argued, the deliberative process exemption serves as an important boundary marking the separation of powers. When congressional oversight "is used as a means of participating directly in an ongoing process of decisionmaking within the Executive Branch, it oversteps the bounds of the proper legislative function."[62]

The executive has also argued that because candor is the principal value served by this category, its protection should extend beyond predecisional deliberations to deliberations involving decisions already made. "Moreover, even if the decision at issue had already been made, disclosure to Congress could still deter the candor of future Executive Branch deliberations."[63] Executives have also taken the position that the privilege covers confidential communications with respect to policymaking well beyond the confines of the White House and the President's closest advisors. The Eisenhower Administration took the most expansive approach, arguing that the privilege applied broadly to advice on official matters among all employees of the executive branch.[64] The Nixon Administration appears to have taken a similar view, arguing that the privilege applied to decision making at a "high governmental level," but conceding that the protected communication must be related to presidential decision making.[65] The Reagan Justice Department appears to have taken a slightly narrower view of the scope of the privilege, requiring that the protected communications have some nexus to the presidential decision-making process.[66]

The George H. W. Bush Administration took the position that recommendations made to senior department officials and communications of senior policymakers throughout the executive branch were protected by executive privilege without regard to whether they involved communications intended to go to the President.[67] The Clinton Administration took a similarly expansive position that all communications within the White House[68] or between the White House and any federal department or agency[69] are presumptively privileged. The George W. Bush Administration, through presidential signing statements,[70] executive orders,[71] and opinions of the

Department of Justice's Office of Legal Counsel (OLC) articulated a legal view of the breadth and reach of presidential constitutional prerogatives that would stymie requests for information and documents often sought by congressional committees.[72] In OLC's view, under the precepts of executive privilege and the unitary executive, Congress may not bypass the procedures the President establishes to authorize disclosure to Congress of classified, privileged, or even non-privileged information by vesting lower-level officers or employees with a right to disclose such information without presidential authorization. Thus, OLC has declared that "right of disclosure" statutes "unconstitutionally limit the ability of the President and his appointees to supervise and control the work of subordinate officers and employees of the Executive Branch."[73] The OLC's assertions of these broad notions of presidential prerogatives are unaccompanied by any authoritative judicial citations. The Obama Administration has only rarely taken formal positions on executive privilege. As such there is limited evidence with which to glean the administration's view of the privilege. On his first day in office President Obama narrowed the scope of executive privilege with respect to former Presidents by revoking and replacing an executive order issued by President George W. Bush relating to a former president's authority to invoke executive privilege over records released under the Presidential Records Act by the Archivist of the United States.[74] Whereas the Bush executive order required the approval of both the former and current President before release of past presidential documents, the Obama executive order does not require the former president to concur in the final determination of whether the documents may be disclosed, and therefore vests ultimate decision making in the current administration.[75] Like past administrations, the Obama administration has utilized signing statements to object to various statutory provisions pertaining to Congress's authority to obtain information from the executive branch.[76] Yet, the Obama signing statements have not referred to "executive privilege" by name as the legal justification for the objection. The context of a number of signing statements, however, indicates that executive privilege is, at least in part, the legal doctrine being asserted.[77]

Executive Acknowledged Limits of the Privilege

The executive branch has acknowledged some limits to its use of executive privilege. Thus, Presidents have stated they will not use executive privilege to block congressional inquiries into allegations of fraud, corruption, or other illegal or unethical conduct in the executive branch. The Clinton Administration announced that "[i]n circumstances involving communications relating to investigations of personal wrongdoing by government officials, it is our practice not to assert executive privilege, either in judicial proceedings or in congressional investigations and hearings."[78] Similarly, the Reagan Administration policy was to refuse to invoke executive privilege when faced with allegations of illegal or unethical conduct: "[T]he privilege should not be invoked to conceal evidence of wrongdoing or criminality on the part of executive officers."[79] A significant application of this policy came in the Iran/Contra investigations when President Reagan did not assert executive privilege and even made "relevant excerpts" of his personal diaries available to congressional investigators.[80]

The executive has often tied its willingness to forgo assertions of executive privilege to the deliberative process exemption from disclosure that it recognizes, stating that it would not seek to protect materials whose disclosure "would not implicate or hinder" the executive decision-making processes.[81] Thus, "factual, nonsensitive materials—communications from the Attorney General [or other executive branch official] which do not contain advice, recommendations, tentative legal judgments, drafts of documents, or other material reflecting deliberative or policymaking processes—do not fall within the scope of materials for which executive privilege may be claimed as a basis of nondisclosure."[82]

Accommodations Reached Between the Executive and Congress

Recent administrations have stated that their policy "is to comply with congressional requests for information to the fullest extent consistent with the constitutional and statutory obligations of the Executive Branch."[83] Therefore, executive privilege will be invoked only after "careful review"[84] in the "most compelling circumstances,"[85] and only after the executive has done "the utmost to reach an accommodation" with Congress.[86] The George W. Bush Administration limited the formal claims of executive privilege to those instances where the effort to accommodate had failed and Congress had issued a subpoena.[87] The duty to seek an accommodation is said to have been the result of the uncertain boundaries between executive and legislative interests.[88] This uncertainty imposes upon each of the branches an "obligation ... to accommodate the legitimate needs of the other,"[89] and a duty to conduct "good faith" negotiations.[90] Avoiding the disclosure of embarrassing information is not a sufficient reason to withhold information from Congress.[91] In fact, it has been asserted that invocation of the privilege should not even be considered in the absence of a "demonstrable justification that Executive withholding will further the public interest."[92]

Where negotiations have faltered and the President has made a formal claim of executive privilege, the executive will likely argue (as the Clinton Administration did in its invocations of executive privilege)[93] that the investigating committee has not made the showing required to overcome the privilege under *Senate Select Committee v. Nixon*: that the subpoenaed evidence is "demonstrably critical to the responsible fulfillment of the Committee's functions."[94] As indicated above, since at least the Reagan Administration, each Administration has argued that Congress's interest in executive information is less compelling when the Committee is exercising its oversight authority rather than considering specific legislative proposals.

Executive Attempts to Expand Executive Privilege

Merging the Presidential Communications Privilege with the Deliberative Process Privilege

Without further judicial consideration of executive privilege since the Nixon cases, the executive, through presidential signing statements, executive orders, OLC Opinions, and, most recently, White House Counsel directives, has attempted to effect a practical expansion of the scope of the privilege. The key vehicle has been the notion of deliberative process. The idea of the deliberative process privilege was developed under the Freedom of Information Act (FOIA) to provide limited protection for communications and documents evidencing the predecisional considerations of agency officials. Over time, the executive branch has melded this deliberative process idea with the recognized confidentiality interest in the President's communications with close advisors, such that the privilege would extend to any policy deliberations or communications within the executive branch in which the President may have an interest.

For example, the legal justifications asserted by the Obama Administration for withholding documents from Congress during a House probe into "Operation Fast and Furious"[95] appear to reflect a heavy reliance on the deliberative process privilege. In a letter to the President asking him to invoke executive privilege over the subpoenaed documents, Attorney General

Eric Holder noted that "Presidents have repeatedly asserted executive privilege to protect confidential Executive Branch deliberative materials from congressional subpoena."[96] The Attorney General went on to argue that "[i]t is well established that 'the doctrine of executive privilege ... encompasses Executive Branch deliberative communications.'"[97] The Attorney General's memorandum made no mention of a distinction between the deliberative process privilege and the presidential communications privilege; nor did the memorandum reference the D.C. Circuit cases of *Espy* and *Judicial Watch*.

Procedures Employed to Assess Potential Privilege Claims

Under the Reagan Administration, if the head of an agency, with the advice of agency counsel, decided that a congressional information request raised substantial questions, the Attorney General, through the Office of Legal Counsel and the White House Counsel's Office, was promptly notified and consulted. If one or more of these advisors deemed the issue substantial, the President was informed, made a decision, and the agency head informed Congress of that decision. The Reagan memo pinpointed national security, deliberative communications that form part of the decision-making process, and other information important to the discharge of executive branch constitutional responsibilities as covered by the privilege.[98] This definition was far narrower than his successors' understanding of the privilege.

The Clinton Administration sought to expand the doctrine by centralizing scrutiny and control of all potential claims of executive privilege in the White House Counsel's Office. The White House Counsel instructed all agency heads to notify his office directly of congressional requests for "any document created in the White House ... or in a department or agency, that contains deliberations of, or advice to or from the White House" that may raise privilege issues. The White House Counsel is to seek an accommodation and if unsuccessful, consult with the Attorney General to determine whether to recommend invocation of the privilege to the President. The President then determines whether to claim privilege, which is then communicated to Congress by the White House Counsel.[99]

Establishing the White House Counsel's Office as a central clearinghouse for presidential privilege claims appears to have had the effect of diminishing the historic role of the Justice Department's Office of Legal Counsel as the constitutional counselor to the President and limiting agencies' ability to deal informally with their congressional overseers, which is likely to have been its principal objective. An apparent consequence during the Clinton years was a more rapid escalation of individual interbranch information disputes clashes, a widening and hardening of the differences in the legal positions of the branches on privilege issues, and an increased difficulty in resolving disputes informally and quickly. President Clinton formally asserted executive privilege fourteen times and resolved a number of disputes under the pressure of imminent committee actions on subpoena issuances and contempt citations.[100] In addition, the Clinton Administration litigated, and lost, significant privilege cases in 1997 and 1998.[101] The first case, *Espy*, arguably undermines many key executive assumptions about the privilege just detailed and thus may reshape the nature and course of future presidential privilege disputes.

IMPLICATIONS AND POTENTIAL IMPACT OF D.C. CIRCUIT PRECEDENT ON FUTURE EXECUTIVE PRIVILEGE DISPUTES

Espy

In *Espy,*[102] the appeals court addressed several important issues left unresolved by the Watergate cases: the precise parameters of the presidential executive privilege; how far down the chain of command the privilege reaches; whether the President has to have seen or had knowledge of the existence of the documents for which he claims privilege; and what showing is necessary to overcome a valid claim of privilege.

The case arose out of an Office of Independent Counsel (OIC) investigation of former Agriculture Secretary Mike Espy. When allegations of improprieties against Espy surfaced in March of 1994, President Clinton ordered the White House Counsel's Office to investigate and report to him so he could determine what action, if any, he should undertake. The White House Counsel's Office prepared a report for the President, which was publicly released on October 11, 1994. The *Espy* court noted that the President never saw any of the report's underlying or supporting documents. Espy had announced his resignation on October 3, to be effective on December 31. The Independent Counsel was appointed on September 9 and the grand jury issued a subpoena for all documents that were accumulated or used in preparation of the report on October 14, three days after the report's issuance. The President withheld 84 documents, claiming both types of executive privilege for all documents. A motion to compel was resisted on the basis of the claimed privilege. After *in camera* review, the district court quashed the subpoena, but in its written opinion the court did not discuss the documents in any detail and provided no analysis of the grand jury's need for the documents. The appeals court panel unanimously reversed.

At the outset, the appeals court's opinion carefully distinguished between the "presidential communications privilege" and the "deliberative process privilege." Both, the court observed, are executive privileges designed to protect the confidentiality of executive branch decision making. But the deliberative process privilege, that applies to executive branch officials generally, is a common law privilege which requires a lower threshold of need to be overcome, and "disappears altogether when there is any reason to believe government misconduct has occurred."[103]

On the other hand, the court explained, the presidential communications privilege is rooted in "constitutional separation of powers principles and the President's unique constitutional role" and applies only to "direct decisionmaking by the President."[104] The privilege may be overcome only by a substantial showing that "the subpoenaed materials likely contain[] important evidence" and that "the evidence is not available with due diligence elsewhere."[105] The presidential communications privilege applies to all documents in their entirety,[106] including pre- and post-decisional materials.[107]

Turning to the chain of command issue, the court held that the presidential communications privilege covers communications made or received by presidential advisers in the course of preparing advice for the President even if those communications are not made directly to the President. The court rested its conclusion on "the President's dependence on presidential advisers and the inability of the deliberative process privilege to provide advisers with adequate freedom from the public spotlight" and "the need to provide sufficient elbow room for advisers to obtain information from all knowledgeable sources."[108] Thus the privilege will "apply both to communications which these advisers solicited and received from others as well as those they authored themselves. The privilege must also extend to communications authored or received in response to a solicitation by members of a presidential adviser's staff."[109]

The court, however, was acutely aware of the dangers of a limitless extension of the privilege to the principles of an open and transparent government. Therefore, it carefully restricted the privilege's reach by explicitly confining it to White House staff that has "operational proximity" to direct presidential decision making. The court held that the privilege did not apply to executive agency staff:

> We are aware that such an extension, unless carefully circumscribed to accomplish the purposes of the privilege, could pose a significant risk of expanding to a large swath of the executive branch a privilege that is bottomed on a recognition of the unique role of the President. In order to limit this risk, the presidential communications privilege should be construed as narrowly as is consistent with ensuring that the confidentiality of the President's decisionmaking process is adequately protected. Not every person who plays a role in the development of presidential advice, no matter how remote and removed from the President, can qualify for the privilege. In particular, the privilege should not extend to staff outside the White House in executive branch agencies. Instead, the privilege should apply only to communications authored or solicited and received by those members of an immediate White House advisor's staff who have broad and significant responsibility for investigation and formulating the advice to be given the President on the particular matter to which the communications relate. Only communications at that level are close enough to the President to be revelatory of his deliberations or to pose a risk to the candor of his advisers. *See* AAPS, 997 F.2d at 910 (it is "operational proximity" to the President that matters in determining whether "[t]he President's confidentiality interests" is implicated) (emphasis omitted).
>
> Of course, the privilege only applies to communications that these advisers and their staff author or solicit and receive in the course of performing their function of advising the President on official government matters. This restriction is particularly important in regard to those officials who exercise substantial independent authority or perform other functions in addition to advising the President, and thus are subject to FOIA and other open government statutes. See *Armstrong v. Executive Office of the President,* 90 F.3d 553, 558 (D.C. Cir. 1996), *cert denied*—U.S.—, 117 S.Ct. 1842, 137 L. Ed.2d 1046 (1997). The presidential communications privilege should never serve as a means of shielding information regarding governmental operations that do not call ultimately for direct decisionmaking by the President. If the government seeks to assert the presidential communications privilege in regard to particular communications of these "dual hat" presidential advisers, the government bears the burden of proving that the communications occurred in conjunction with the process of advising the President.[110]

Because the appeals court limited the presidential communications privilege to "direct decisionmaking by the President," it is important to identify the type of decision making the subpoenaed documents or requested information implicates. Arguably, the opinion restricts the scope of the privilege to encompass only those functions that form the core of presidential authority, involving what the court characterized as "quintessential and non-delegable Presidential power."[111]

In the case before it, the court was specifically addressing the President's Article II appointment and removal power, which was the focus of the advice he sought from the White House Counsel in the Espy matter. However, it seems clear from the context of the opinion that the description was meant to juxtapose non-delegable powers, such as the appointment and removal power, with other presidential powers that "can be exercised or performed without the President's direct involvement, pursuant to a presidential delegation of authority or statutory framework."[112] The court illustrated the latter category by pointing to the President's Article II duty "to take care that the laws are faithfully executed." The courts have consistently held that this constitutional instruction is not a source of presidential power, but rather the President's obligation to ensure that the will of Congress is carried out by the executive bureaucracy.[113]

Although not expressly and unequivocally establishing such a requirement, it appears that the appeals court may have limited the application of the newly formulated presidential communications privilege to Article II functions that are "quintessential and non-delegable."[114] This category appears to include the appointment and removal powers, the commander-in-chief power, the sole authority to receive ambassadors and other public ministers, the power to negotiate treaties, and the power to grant pardons and reprieves. Decision making vested by statute in the President or agency heads such as rulemaking, environmental policy, consumer protection, workplace safety and labor relations, among others, may not necessarily be covered by the privilege. Of course, the President's role in supervising and coordinating decision making in the executive branch remains unimpeded, but his communications in furtherance of such activities may not be protected by the constitutional privilege.

Such a reading of this critical passage of the court's opinion conforms with the court's view of the source and purpose of the presidential communications privilege and the need to define it narrowly. Relying on *Nixon I,* the *Espy* court identified "the President's Article II powers and responsibilities as the constitutional basis of the presidential communications privilege ... Since the Constitution assigns these responsibilities to the President alone, arguably the privilege of confidentiality that derives from it also should be the President's alone."[115] Again relying on *Nixon* I, the court pinpointed the essential purpose of the privilege:

deliberative process privilege would have to suffice.[131] The majority found that privilege insufficient and ordered the disclosure of the 4,300 withheld documents.

Committee on the Judiciary v. Miers

The important 2008 district court opinion in *Committee on the Judiciary v. Miers* has also played a role in defining the outer contours of executive privilege. In early 2007, the House Judiciary Committee and its Subcommittee on Commercial and Administrative Law commenced an inquiry into the termination and replacement of a number of United States Attorneys. Six hearings and numerous interviews were conducted by the committees between March and June 2007, focusing on the actions of present and former Department of Justice (DOJ) officials and employees as well as related DOJ documents. On March 21, 2007, the House Subcommittee authorized Chairman John Conyers, Jr. to issue subpoenas to a number of present and former White House officials for documents and testimony. On June 13, 2007, Chairman Conyers issued subpoenas to White House Chief of Staff Joshua Bolten, in his role as custodian of White House documents, and to former White House Counsel Harriet Miers.

On June 27, 2007, White House Counsel Fred F. Fielding, at the direction of President Bush, wrote to the Chairmen of the House and Senate Judiciary Committees regarding the document subpoenas issued to Mr. Bolten and Ms. Miers. Fielding notified the committees that the President was asserting executive privilege and had instructed the subpoena recipients not to produce any documents. Additionally, the Fielding letter noted that the testimony sought from Ms. Miers was also subject to a "valid claim of Executive Privilege," and would be asserted if the matter could not be resolved before the scheduled appearance date.[132]

Accompanying the Fielding letter was a legal memorandum prepared by Acting Attorney General Paul D. Clement, for the President, detailing the legal basis for a claim of executive privilege.[133] The memo identified three categories of documents being sought by the committee: (1) internal White House communications; (2) communications by White House officials with individuals outside the executive branch, including individuals in the Legislative Branch; and (3) communications between White House and Justice Department officials.[134] Internal White House communications included discussions of "the wisdom" of removal and replacement proposals, which

U.S. Attorneys should be removed, and possible responses to Congressional and media inquiries. The memo claimed these discussions were the "types of internal deliberations among White House officials [that] fall squarely within the scope of executive privilege" since their nondisclosure "promote[s] sound decisionmaking by ensuring that senior Government officials and their advisors may speak frankly and candidly during the decisionmaking process."[135] Furthermore, the memo argued that the President's protected confidentiality interests "are particularly" strong in this instance because the presidential power to appoint and remove officers of the United States is a "quintessential and nondelegable Presidential power."[136] As a consequence, an inquiring committee would have to meet the standard established by the *Senate Select Committee* decision, showing that the documents and information are "demonstrably critical to the responsible fulfillment of the Committee's function," to overcome the privilege and achieve disclosure.[137]

On June 29, 2007, Chairman Conyers and Senate Judiciary Committee Chairman Patrick Leahy jointly responded to the Fielding letter and Clement memo. Characterizing the White House stance as "based on blanket executive privilege claims," which makes it difficult for the Committees "to determine where privilege truly does and does not apply," the Committees demanded that they be provided with a detailed privilege log. The log was to include the following information for each document withheld: a description of the nature, source, subject matter and date of the document; the name and address of each recipient of an original or copy of the document and the date received; the name and address of each additional person to whom any of the contents of the document was disclosed, along with the date and manner of disclosure; and the specific basis for the assertion of privilege. A deadline for receipt of the privilege log was set for July 9, 2007.

On July 9, 2007, the White House Counsel refused to comply. On that same date, counsel to Ms. Miers informed Chairman Conyers that, pursuant to letters received from the White House Counsel, Miers would not answer questions or produce documents. The next day Ms. Miers' counsel announced that she would not appear at all. Also on July 10, the DOJ Office of Legal Counsel (OLC) issued an opinion stating that "Ms. Miers is [absolutely] immune from compulsion to testify before the Committee on this matter and therefore is not required to appear to testify about the subject."[138] Citing previous OLC opinions, the opinion asserted that since the President is the head of one of the independent branches of the federal government, "If a congressional committee could force the President's appearance, fundamental separation of powers principles—including the President's independence and autonomy from Congress— would be threatened."[139] Consequently, "[t]he same separation of powers principles that protect a President from compelled congressional testimony also apply to senior presidential advisors" because such appearances would be tantamount to the President himself appearing.[140] The fact that Ms. Miers was a former counsel to the President would not alter the analysis since, in OLC's view, "a presidential advisor's immunity is derivative of the President's." Neither Ms. Miers nor Mr. Bolten complied with the subpoenas by the return dates.

On July 12 and July 19 the House Subcommittee met and Chairman Sánchez issued a ruling rejecting both Ms. Miers' and Mr. Bolton's privilege claims. On July 25, the full Judiciary Committee voted, 21-17, to issue a report to the House recommending that a resolution of contempt of Congress against Ms. Miers and Mr. Bolten be approved. Thereafter, the White House announced that it would order the U.S. Attorney for the District of Columbia not to present the contempt of Congress citation for grand jury consideration.[141]

The Judiciary Committee filed its report formally reporting a contempt violation to the House in November 2007.[142] After further attempts at accommodation failed, the matter was brought to the floor of the House on February 14, 2008. The House voted 223 to 32[143] in favor of two resolutions.[144] House Resolution 979 directed the Speaker to certify the Judiciary Committee report, detailing Ms. Miers' refusal to appear, testify, or produce documents for the Committee and Mr. Bolten's refusal to produce documents, in violation of the subpoenas, to the U.S.

Attorney for the District of Columbia for presentation to a grand jury pursuant to 2 U.S.C. §§ 192 and 194.[145] House Resolution 980 was passed in apparent anticipation that the U.S. Attorney would not present the criminal contempt citation to the grand jury. The resolution authorized the Chairman of the Judiciary Committee to initiate civil judicial proceedings in federal court to seek a declaratory judgment affirming the duty of any individual to comply with any subpoena that is the subject of House Resolution 979 and to issue appropriate injunctions to achieve compliance. The resolution also authorized the House General Counsel to represent the Committee in any such litigation.

On February 28, 2008, the Speaker certified the Committee's Report to the U.S. Attorney. The next day, however, Attorney General Mukasey advised the Speaker that "the Department will not bring the congressional contempt citations before a grand jury or take any other action to prosecute Mr. Bolten or Ms. Miers."[146]

On March 10, 2008, the House General Counsel filed a civil action for declaratory judgment and injunctive relief against Ms. Miers and Mr. Bolten.[147] The suit sought an order directing Ms. Miers to appear before the Committee, respond to questions, and only invoke executive privilege if appropriate. Additionally, the Committee requested that Ms. Miers and Mr. Bolten provide detailed privilege logs for the documents claimed to be privileged and produce all other documents subject to the subpoenas.[148] Shortly after filing the case, the House General Counsel filed a Motion for Partial Summary Judgment seeking a declaration that (1) Ms. Miers failure to appear at all in response to the Committee's subpoena was without legal justification; (2) that she must appear before the Committee and can assert privilege claims in response to questions, as appropriate, but must testify about subjects not covered by privilege; (3) that the failure of both Ms. Miers and Mr. Bolten to supply privilege logs with respect to withheld documents is legally unjustified; and (4) that both be ordered to provide detailed privilege logs with respect to documents claimed to be privileged and to produce all relevant non-privileged documents.[149] In opposition, the Executive argued that the suit should be dismissed because the Committee lacked standing and a cause of action.[150] Furthermore, it argued that the court should not involve itself in disputes between the political branches that have traditionally been resolved through direct negotiation.[151]

On July 31, 2008, the district court essentially granted the Committee's motion for partial summary judgment in its entirety.[152] In its lengthy opinion, the court rejected the executive's justiciability claims, finding both standing and an implied cause of action in the Constitution's institutional commitment to Congress in Article I of "the power of inquiry." It noted that the Supreme Court has consistently recognized that this power carries with it an enforcement mechanism, which is "an essential and appropriate auxiliary to the legislative function."[153] Furthermore, the court stated that "issuance of a subpoena pursuant to an authorized investigation is ... an indispensable ingredient of law making."[154] In rejecting the suggestion that the court exercise its equitable discretion not to adjudicate an inter-branch political dispute, the court observed that many courts since the initial Watergate rulings deemed it appropriate to attempt to resolve subpoena disputes. These disputes, both civil and criminal, involved privilege claims in circumstances where it appeared only judicial intervention could "prevent a stalemate ... that could result in a paralysis of government operations."[155] The court noted that both parties conceded that they were at an impasse and observed:

> Although the identity of the litigants in this case necessitates that the Court proceed with caution, that is not a convincing reason to decline to decide a case that presents important legal questions. Rather than running roughshod over separation of powers principles, the Court believes that entertaining this case will reinforce them. Two parties cannot negotiate in good faith when one side asserts legal privileges but insists that they cannot be tested in court in the traditional manner. That is true whether the negotiating parties are private firms or the political branches of the federal government. Accordingly, the Court will deny the Executive's motion to dismiss.[156]

Turning to the executive's claim that present and past senior advisers to the President are absolutely immune from compelled congressional process, the court rejected the executive's position:

> The Executive cannot identify a single judicial opinion that recognizes absolute immunity for senior presidential advisors in this or any other context. That simple yet critical fact bears repeating: the asserted absolute immunity claim here is entirely unsupported by existing case law. In fact, there is Supreme Court authority that is all but conclusive on this question and that powerfully suggests that such advisors do not enjoy absolute immunity. The Court therefore rejects the Executive's claim of absolute immunity for senior presidential aides.[157]

At the outset, the court noted that the 1950 Supreme Court ruling in *United States v. Bryan*[158] established that if a congressional subpoena requirement is ignored, "the great power of testimonial compulsion, so necessary to the effective functioning of courts and legislatures, would be a nullity."[159] In attempting to explain why it should not have to comply here, the executive argued that since the President is absolutely immune to compelled congressional testimony, close advisers to the President must be regarded as his "alter ego" and, therefore, be entitled to the same absolute immunity. The court responded that the same line of argument was rejected by the Supreme Court in *Harlow v. Fitzgerald*,[160] a suit for damages against senior White House aides arising out of the defendants' official actions. The aides claimed they were "entitled to a blanket protection of absolute immunity as an incident of their offices as Presidential aides."[161] Recognizing that absolute immunity had been extended to legislators, judges, prosecutors, and the President himself, the Supreme Court rejected extending such immunity further, emphasizing that "[f]or executive officials in general, however, our cases make plain that qualified immunity represents the norm."[162] The Court rejected the argument that it had accorded derivative immunity to legislative aides in Speech or Debate cases as "sweep[ing] too far," noting that even cabinet members "are not entitled to absolute immunity."[163] The *Harlow* Court did concede that a presidential aide could have absolute immunity if the responsibilities of his office included a sensitive function, such as foreign policy or national security, and he was discharging the protected functions when performing the act for which liability is asserted.[164] The *Miers* district court concluded that in this matter, since there was no involvement of national security or foreign policy concerns, neither Ms. Miers' nor Mr. Bolten's close proximity to the President was sufficient under *Harlow* to provide either absolute or qualified immunity.[165]

In response to the Executive's claim that without absolute immunity there would be a "chilling effect" on the candid and frank advice advisers would provide a Chief Executive, the court stated:

> The prospect of being hauled in front of Congress – daunting as it may be – would not necessarily trigger the chilling effect that the Executive predicts. Senior executive officials often testify before Congress as a normal part of their jobs, and forced testimony before Congress does not implicate the same concern regarding personal financial exposure as does a damages suit. Significantly, the Committee concedes that an executive branch official may assert executive privilege on a question-by-question basis as appropriate. That should serve as an effective check against public disclosure of truly privileged communications, thereby mitigating any adverse impact on the quality of advice that the President receives ... . In any event, the historical record produced by the Committee reveals that senior advisors to the President have often testified before Congress subject to various subpoenas dating back to 1973. Thus, it would hardly be unprecedented for Ms. Miers to appear before Congress to testify and assert executive privilege where appropriate. Still, it is noteworthy that in an environment where there is no judicial support whatsoever for the Executive's claim of absolute immunity, the historical record also does not reflect the wholesale compulsion by Congress of testimony from senior presidential advisors that the Executive fears.[166]

Next, the district court rejected the claim that *Nixon I* established that a president's immunity is qualified, and not absolute, only when judicial resolution of a criminal justice matter was at stake.[167] The executive argued that this case involved only a "peripheral" exercise of Congress's power, not a core function of another branch. The court responded:

> Congress's power of inquiry is as broad as its power to legislate and lies at the very heart of Congress's constitutional role. Indeed, the former is necessary to the proper exercise of the latter: according to the Supreme Court, the ability to compel testimony is "*necessary to the effective functioning of courts and legislatures*." *Bryan* 339 U.S. at 331 (emphasis added). Thus, Congress's use of (and need for vindication of) its subpoena power in this case is not less legitimate or important than was the grand jury's in *United States v. Nixon*. Both involve core functions of a co-equal branch of the federal government, and for the reasons identified in *Nixon*, the President may only be entitled to a presumptive, rather than absolute, privilege here. And it is certainly the case that if the President is entitled only to a presumptive privilege, his close advisors cannot hold the superior card of absolute immunity... [A] claim of absolute immunity from compulsory process cannot be erected by the Executive as a surrogate for the claim of absolute privilege already firmly rejected by the courts. Presidential autonomy, such as it is, cannot mean that the Executive's actions are totally insulated from scrutiny by Congress. That would eviscerate the Congress's oversight functions.[168]

The court recognized that claiming that close presidential advisors were entitled to absolute privilege made the President the judge of the parameters of his own privilege. The court concluded that such a power "would impermissibly transform the presumptive privilege into an absolute one, yet that is what the Executive seeks through its assertion of Ms. Miers absolute immunity from compulsory process. That proposition is untenable and cannot be justified by appeals to Presidential autonomy."[169]

Finally, the district court rejected the Executive's fall-back position: that even if Ms. Miers is not entitled to absolute immunity, she should be accorded qualified immunity. The court dismissed the argument, relying on the analysis established by *Harlow*:

> [T]his inquiry does not involve sensitive topics of national security or foreign affairs. Congress, moreover, is acting pursuant to a legitimate use of its investigative authority. Notwithstanding its best efforts, the Committee has been unable to discover the underlying causes of the forced terminations of the U.S. Attorneys. The Committee has legitimate reasons to believe that Ms. Miers's testimony can remedy that deficiency.

> There is no evidence that the Committee is merely seeing to harass Ms. Miers by calling her to testify. Importantly, moreover, Ms. Miers remains able to assert privilege in response to any specific question or subject matter. For its part, the Executive has not offered any independent reasons that Ms. Miers should be relieved from compelled congressional testimony beyond its blanket assertion of absolute immunity. The Executive's showing, then, does not support either absolute or qualified immunity in this case.[170]

The Administration appealed the district court decision and asked the U.S. Court of Appeals for the District of Columbia Circuit (D.C. Circuit) to stay the district court order pending an expedited final decision by that court. On September 16, 2008 the D.C. Circuit granted the stay, but denied the Administration's request for an expedited schedule.[171] The appeals court had concluded that "even if expedited, this controversy will not be fully and finally resolved by the Judicial Branch ... before the 110th Congress ends on January 3, 2009. At that time, the 110th House of Representatives will cease to exist as a legal entity, and the subpoenas it has issued will expire."[172] Accordingly, because the Committee's subpoenas were likely to expire before the dispute could be resolved, the court saw no reason to expedite the case.[173]

On January 13, 2009—with the *Miers* case still on appeal before the D.C. Circuit, the 110th Congress having reached its conclusion, and all presidential records set to transfer into the custody of the Archivist of the United States[174] at the end of President Bush's second term on January 20th—the district court issued a second order to preserve the availability of documents covered by the Committee subpoenas.[175] The order required the Administration to make copies of all materials responsive to the subpoenas for storage at the White House until the conclusion of the litigation.

In March of 2009, after the arrival of a newly elected Congress and presidential administration, the parties reached a settlement in which some, but not all, of the requested documents would be provided to the Committee. In addition, Ms. Miers would be permitted to testify, under oath, in a closed, but transcribed hearing.[176] Accordingly, the D.C. Circuit dismissed *Miers* on October 14, 2009, pursuant to a motion for voluntary dismissal.[177] Thus, the Miers litigation ended more than a year and a half after the Committee first filed its suit to enforce the subpoenas. Ultimately, however, the Committee was able to gain access to much of the information it had been seeking.[178]

Although the district court opinion in *Miers* is perhaps best characterized as a vindication of congressional oversight prerogatives, or at least a clear limitation on the scope of executive privilege in the face of a congressional investigation, the ultimate impact of the case is unclear. The reasoning adopted by the court may have significant influence in that it so clearly repudiated the executive's claim of absolute immunity for presidential advisors, while reaffirming Congress's essential role in conducting oversight and enforcing its own subpoenas. However, the impact of the ruling may also be limited by the fact that, as a district court decision, it carries only the precedential weight that its reasoning may bear. Moreover, the case did not provide any discussion of the merits of Miers' specific claims of executive privilege, but rather held that although not enjoying absolute immunity from congressionally compelled testimony, Ms. Miers was still free to assert executive privilege "in response to any specific questions posed by the Committee."[179] Thus, Ms. Miers could still assert the protections of executive privilege during her testimony depending on the substance of any individual question posed by a Member of the Committee. Finally, the court also suggested, without further explanation, that Congress may lack authority to compel testimony where such testimony related to national security, foreign affairs, or another "particularly sensitive function" of the executive branch.[180]

Loving v. Department of Defense

In *Loving v. Department of Defense*, the D.C. Circuit reaffirmed the distinction between the deliberative process privilege and the presidential communications privilege that had been carefully explained in *Espy* and *Judicial Watch*.[181] The *Loving* court held that the presidential communications privilege applies only where documents or communications "directly involve the President" or were "solicited and received" by White House advisors.[182] The case was precipitated by a FOIA request filed by army private Dwight Loving seeking disclosure of various documents, including a Department of Defense memorandum containing recommendations to the President about Loving's murder conviction by a military tribunal and subsequent death sentence. After noting the two distinct versions of executive privilege,[183] the appeals court determined that the documents in question were indeed protected from disclosure as they fell "squarely within the presidential communications privilege because they 'directly involve' the President."[184] The court also clarified that communications that "directly involve" the President, need not actually be "solicited and received" by him. The mere fact that the documents were viewed by the President was sufficient to bring them within the privilege.[185] It is important to note that in its relatively brief discussion of the presidential communications privilege, the *Loving* court did not reference the discussion of "non-delegable presidential duties" that was included in *Espy* and *Judicial Watch*.

PRESIDENT OBAMA'S ASSERTION OF EXECUTIVE PRIVILEGE

On June 20, 2012, Deputy Attorney General James Cole alerted the House Committee on Oversight and Government Reform that President Obama was asserting executive privilege over documents subpoenaed by the committee during its ongoing investigation of Operation Fast and Furious. This assertion appears to be the first time President Obama has formally invoked executive privilege.

Operation Fast and Furious Investigation

In January 2011, the Senate Judiciary Committee began investigating the Bureau of Alcohol, Tobacco, Firearms, and Explosives (ATF) and DOJ regarding Operation Fast and Furious,[186] an ATF operation based in the Phoenix, Arizona field office.

ATF whistleblowers alleged that suspected straw purchasers[187] were allowed to amass large quantities of firearms as part of longterm gun trafficking investigations.[188] As a consequence, some of these firearms were allegedly "walked,"[189] or trafficked, to gunrunners and other criminals, and some were smuggled into Mexico.[190]

In December 2010, two of these firearms were reportedly found at the scene of a shootout, near the U.S.-Mexico border, where U.S. Border Patrol Agent Brian Terry was shot to death.[191] Following public reports of the Operation and Agent Terry's death, Attorney General Eric Holder instructed the DOJ Office of Inspector General to review ATF's gun trafficking investigations.[192]

On February 4, 2011, Assistant Attorney General Ronald Weich sent a letter to Senator Grassley, ranking Member of the Senate Judiciary Committee, denying that the ATF had sanctioned or knew of the sale of weapons to straw purchasers who then transported them into Mexico.[193] In March 2011, the

House Committee on Oversight and Government Reform began their own investigation of Operation Fast and Furious. Representative Darrell Issa, Chairman of the Oversight Committee, requested documents and information about the Operation from then-Acting ATF Director Kenneth E. Melson. The Department of Justice responded to the request but, according to the committee, "did not provide any documents or information to the Committee by the March 30, 2011 deadline."[194] The following day, the committee issued a subpoena to DOJ and ATF.[195] Over the next year, the Oversight and Government Reform Committee held several hearings regarding Operation Fast and Furious,[196] and Attorney General Holder testified before that Committee as well as the House and Senate Judiciary and Appropriations Committees. On October 12, 2011, the Oversight and Government Reform Committee issued a second subpoena to Attorney General Holder, after the DOJ informed the committee that it was done producing documents in response to the first subpoena. This subpoena requested all departmental communications and documents "referring or related to Operation Fast and Furious...." At a November 8, 2011 Senate Judiciary Committee hearing, Attorney General Holder conceded that the February 4, 2011 letter from DOJ to Congress contained "inaccurate" information about the depth of knowledge DOJ officials had regarding ATF's "gun walking" methods.[197] The next month, the DOJ formally withdrew the February 4 letter and acknowledged that Operation Fast and Furious was "fundamentally flawed."[198] The letter was accompanied by nearly 1,400 pages of documents and communications that addressed how inaccurate information had been included in the February 4 letter.[199]

This disclosure deviated from the DOJ's general position that requests like this Committee's, "seeking information about the Executive Branch's deliberations ... implicate significant confidentiality interests grounded in the separation of powers under the U.S. Constitution."[200] Throughout the Committee's investigation into the scope of DOJ's knowledge of Operation Fast and Furious, each party has had different opinions about the nature and extent of DOJ's cooperation in producing subpoenaed documents and communications. The DOJ maintained that it made "extraordinary accommodations"[201] in responding to requests about the drafting of the February 4 letter. Furthermore, it stated:

> The Department has substantially complied with the outstanding subpoenas. The documents responsive to the remaining subpoena items pertain to sensitive law enforcement activities, including ongoing

> criminal investigations and prosecutions, or were generated by Department officials in the course of responding to congressional investigations or media inquiries about this matter that are generally not appropriate for disclosure.[202]

However, the Committee maintains that despite its flexibility and it being "unfailingly patient,"[203] "the Department has refused to produce certain documents"[204] and "has fought this committee's investigation every step of the way."[205] During a committee hearing, Chairman Issa remarked that the Attorney General specifically has "refused to cooperate, offering to provide subpoenaed documents only if the committee agrees in advance to close the investigation. No investigator would ever agree to that."[206] In its contempt committee report, it stated that the DOJ's refusal to cooperate with congressional investigators was "inexcusable and cannot stand."[207]

The Committee's continued dissatisfaction with the DOJ's refusal to comply fully with the subpoenas led it to schedule a vote to hold Attorney General Holder in contempt of Congress. While the Attorney General and Chairman Issa met the night before the scheduled vote, they were unable to reach an acceptable accommodation with regard to document disclosure. On the morning of the vote, President Obama formally invoked executive privilege "over the relevant post-February 4, 2011, documents."[208] In defending this assertion, the DOJ noted that:

> the compelled production to Congress of these internal Executive Branch documents generated in the course of the deliberative process concerning the Department's response to congressional oversight and related media inquiries would have significant, damaging consequences ... it would inhibit the candor of such Executive Branch deliberations in the future and significantly impair the Executive Branch's ability to respond independently and effectively to congressional oversight. Such compelled disclosure would be inconsistent with the separation of powers established in the Constitution and would potentially create an imbalance in the relationship between these co-equal branches of the Government.[209]

In its contempt citation, the Oversight and Government Reform Committee rejected the President's assertion of executive privilege, calling it "transparently invalid" due to the timing and blanket application of the privilege to all withheld documents.[210] The Committee voted 23 to 17 to hold Attorney General Holder in contempt of Congress.[211]

On June 28, 2012, the full House voted to hold him in contempt of Congress, by a vote of 255 to 67.[212]

CONCLUSION

As indicated in the above discussion, recent appellate court rulings cast considerable doubt on the broad claims of privilege posited by the executive branch in the past. Taken together, *Espy* and *Judicial Watch* arguably have affected important qualifications and restraints on the nature, scope and reach of the presidential communications privilege. As established by those cases, and until reviewed by the Supreme Court, the following elements should be considered in determining when the privilege can be invoked properly:

1. The communication must be authored or "solicited and received" by a close White House advisor or the President. The judicial test requires that an advisor be in "operational proximity" to the President. This effectively means that the scope of the presidential communications privilege can extend only to the administrative boundaries of the Executive Office of the President and the White House. It appears not to apply to communications or documents wholly produced within an executive department or agency.
2. The presidential communications privilege may be limited to communications relating to a "quintessential and non-delegable presidential power." *Espy* and *Judicial Watch* involved the appointment and removal and the pardon powers, respectively. Other core, direct presidential decision-making powers include the Commander-in-Chief power, the sole authority to receive ambassadors and other public ministers, and the power to negotiate treaties. However, neither case explicitly stated that the presidential communications privilege could only apply to communications and documents relating to "quintessential and non-delegable presidential power[s]."
3. The presidential communications privilege remains a qualified privilege that may be overcome by a showing that the information sought "likely contains important evidence" and cannot be obtained from other sources. The *Espy* court found an adequate showing of need by the Independent Counsel that overcame the privilege.

In *Judicial Watch*, the court found the presidential communications privilege did not apply, and remanded to the district court to determine if the deliberative process privilege would apply to specific documents.

Definitively applying the teachings of *Espy* and *Judicial Watch* to current information access disputes between Congress and the executive may be premature because these cases were decided in the context of judicial and FOIA requests for information from the executive branch. In the congressional-executive conflict context, it is clear that the *Miers* court unequivocally rejected the claim of absolute witness immunity and adopted the Committee's argument that the Supreme Court's ruling in *Nixon I* allows only a qualified constitutional privilege that may be overcome by a proper showing of need.

Furthermore, the court recognized that subsequent Supreme Court and appellate court rulings have reiterated the qualified nature of the privilege.[213] However, outside of the district court opinion in *Miers*, there is no other post-Watergate case law addressing executive privilege in the congressional-executive dispute context. Indeed, the *Espy* court specifically noted that its narrow holding was limited to the confines of judicial requests for information:

> Finally, we underscore our opinion should not be read as in any way affecting the scope of the privilege in the congressional-executive context, the arena where conflict over the privilege of confidentiality arises most frequently. The President's ability to withhold information from Congress implicates different constitutional considerations than the President's ability to withhold evidence in judicial proceedings. Our determination of how far down into the executive branch the presidential communications privilege goes is limited to the context before us, namely where information generated by close presidential advisers is sought for use in a judicial proceedings, and we take no position on how the institutional needs of Congress and the President should be balanced.[214]

In the continuing absence of a post-Nixon Supreme Court decision and since *Miers* never proceeded to a decision on the merits in the appeals court, there is continuing uncertainty as to how executive privilege claims should be analyzed when asserted in response to congressional requests for information.

Appendix. Presidential Claims of Executive Privilege from the Kennedy Administration through the Obama Administration

The following is a brief summary of assertions of presidential claims of executive privilege from the Kennedy Administration through the Obama Administration.

1. Kennedy

President Kennedy established the policy that he, and he alone, would invoke the privilege. Kennedy appears to have utilized the privilege twice with respect to information requests by congressional committees. In 1962, the President directed the Secretary of Defense not to supply the names of individuals who wrote or edited speeches in response to a request by a Senate subcommittee investigating military Cold War education and speech review policies. The chairman of the subcommittee acquiesced to the assertion. The President also directed his military adviser, General Maxwell Taylor, to refuse to testify before a congressional committee examining the Bay of Pigs affair. *See* Rozell, *supra* note 1, at 40-41.

2. Johnson

Although he announced that he would follow the Kennedy policy of personal assertion of executive privilege, President Johnson did not follow the practice. Rozell, *supra* note 1, at 41-42, catalogues three instances in which executive officials refused to comply with congressional committee requests for information or testimony that involved presidential actions. These executive officials did not claim that the President directed them to assert the privilege.

3. Nixon

President Nixon asserted executive privilege six times. He directed Attorney General Mitchell to withhold FBI reports from a congressional committee in 1970. In 1971, at the President's direction, Secretary of State Rogers asserted privilege and withheld information from Congress about military assistance programs.

A claim of privilege was asserted at the direction of the President to prevent a White House advisor from testifying on the International Telephone and Telegraph (ITT) settlement during the Senate Judiciary Committee's consideration of the Richard Kleindienst nomination for Attorney General in 1972.

Finally, President Nixon claimed executive privilege three times with respect to subpoenas for White House tapes relating to the Watergate affair: one subpoena from the Senate Select Committee; one grand jury subpoena for the same tapes issued by Special Prosecutor Archibald Cox; and one jury trial subpoena for 64 additional tapes issued by Special Prosecutor Leon Jaworski. Rozell, *supra* note 1, at 57-62.

4. Ford and Carter

President Ford directed Secretary of State Henry Kissinger to withhold documents during a congressional committee investigation of State Department recommendations to the National Security Council to conduct covert activities in 1975. President Carter directed Energy Secretary Charles Duncan to claim executive privilege when a committee demanded documents relating to the development and implementation of a policy to impose a petroleum import fee. Rozell, supra note 1, at 77-82, 87-91.

5. Reagan

President Reagan directed the assertion of executive privilege before congressional committees three times: by Secretary of the Interior James Watt with respect to an investigation of Canadian oil leases (1981-82); by EPA Administrator Anne Gorsuch Burford with respect to Superfund enforcement practices (1982-83); and by Justice William Rehnquist during his nomination proceedings for Chief Justice with respect to memos he wrote when he was

Assistant Attorney General for the DOJ Office of Legal Counsel (1986). Rozell, *supra* note 1, at 98-105.

6. Bush, George H. W.

President Bush asserted privilege only once, in 1991, when he ordered Defense Secretary Dick Cheney not to comply with a congressional subpoena for a document related to a subcommittee's investigation of cost overruns in, and cancellation of, a Navy aircraft program. Rozell, *supra* note 1, at 108-19.

7. Clinton

President Clinton apparently discontinued the policy of issuing *written* directives to subordinate officials to exercise executive privilege. Thus, in some instances, it is not completely clear when a subordinate's privilege claim was orally directed by the President, even if it was quickly withdrawn. The following documented assertions may arguably be deemed formal invocations of the privilege. Four of these assertions occurred during grand jury proceedings.

a) Kennedy Notes (1995) (executive privilege initially raised but never formally asserted) (Senate Whitewater investigation). S.Rept. 104-191, 104th Cong., 1st Sess. (1995).
b) White House Counsel Jack Quinn/Travelgate Investigations (1996) (House Government Reform). H.Rept. 104-598, 104th Cong., 2d Sess. (1996).
c) FBI-DEA Drug Enforcement Memo (1996) (House Judiciary).
d) Haiti/Political Assassinations Documents (1996) (House International Relations).
e) In re Grand Jury Subpoena Duces Tecum, 112 F. 3d 910 (8th Cir. 1997) (executive privilege claimed and then withdrawn in the district court. Appeals court rejected applicability of common interest doctrine to communications with White House Counsel's Office attorneys and private attorneys for the First Lady).
f) In re Sealed Case (Espy), 121 F. 3d 729 (D.C. Cir. 1997) (executive privilege asserted but held overcome with respect to documents revealing false statements).

g) In re Grand Jury Proceedings, 5 F. Supp. 2d 21 (D.D.C. 1998) (executive privilege claimed but held overcome because testimony of close advisors was relevant and necessary to grand jury investigation of Lewinski matter and was unavailable elsewhere).

The September 9, 1998, Referral to the House of Representatives by Independent Counsel Kenneth Starr detailed the following previously undisclosed presidential claims of executive privilege (viii - xiii) before grand juries, which occurred during the Independent Counsel's investigations of the Hubbell and Lewinski matters:

h) Thomas "Mack" McLarty (1997) (claimed at direction of President during Hubbell investigation, but withdrawn prior to filing of a motion to compel).
i) Nancy Hernreich (claimed at direction of President, but withdrawn prior to March 20, 1998 hearing to compel).
j) Sidney Blumenthal (claim rejected by district court, In re Grand Jury Proceedings, 5 F. Supp. 2d 21 (D.D.C. 1998), and dropped on appeal).
k) Cheryl Mills (claimed on August 11, 1998).
l) Lanny Breuer (claimed on August 4, 1998 and denied by Judge Johnson on August 11). In re Grand Jury Proceeding. Unpublished Order (Under Seal) (August 11, 1998).
m) Bruce Lindsey (claimed on August 28, 1998). H.Doc. 105-310, 105th Cong, 2d Sess. 206- 09 (1998).
n) FALN Clemency (claimed at direction of President by Deputy Counsel to the President Cheryl Mills on September 16, 1999 in response to subpoenas by House Committee on Government Reform).

8. Bush, George W.

President Bush asserted executive privilege six times, using both written and oral directives to subordinate executive officials to claim the privilege.

1. On December 12, 2001, President Bush ordered Attorney General John Ashcroft not to comply with a congressional subpoena for documents related to a House Committee's investigation of corruption in the FBI's Boston regional office. The documents were ultimately

released shortly after the Committee held oversight hearings. H.Rept. 108-414, 108th Cong., 1st Sess. (2004).

2. *Judicial Watch Inc. v. Dep't of Justice*, 365 F.3d. 1108 (D.C. Cir. 2004) (rejecting the claimed applicability of the presidential communications privilege to pardon documents sought under FOIA from DOJ's Office of the Pardon Attorney).
3. Removal and Replacement of U.S. Attorneys (2007). At the direction of the President, on June 28, 2007, the White House Counsel advised the House and Senate Judiciary Committees that subpoenas issued to former White House Counsel Harriet Miers and Chief of Staff Joshua B. Bolten for documents and testimony relating to the firing of U.S. Attorneys were subject to a claim of executive privilege. Additionally, these present and former White House officials were ordered not to comply with document demands or appear at a hearing. The House passed contempt resolutions against Miers and Bolten on February 14, 2008. On February 28, the Speaker transmitted the contempt citation to the U.S. Attorney for the District of Columbia for presentation to the grand jury. The Attorney General directed the U.S. Attorney not to present the citation. On March 10, 2008, the House Judiciary Committee initiated a civil suit seeking declaratory and injunctive relief to enforce the subpoenas. See Comm. on the Judiciary, U.S. House of Representatives v. Miers, 558 F. Supp. 2d 53 (D.D.C. 2008). On July 31, 2008, the district court ruled that "The Executive's current claim of absolute immunity from compelled congressional process for senior precedential aides is without any support in the case law." Id. at 56. The court declared that Ms. Miers was legally required to testify after being issued a valid congressional subpoena and ordered Ms. Miers and Mr. Bolten to produce all subpoenaed non-privileged documents. Additionally, while stopping short of ordering production of a full privilege log, the court did require the executive to provide more detailed descriptions of all documents withheld on the basis of executive privilege. Id. at 107. The appeals court stayed the district court order pending appeal, but the appeals court never issued a ruling on the merits because an accommodation was reached before it could take up the case. Following the expiration of the 110th Congress and the arrival of a new administration, the parties reached an agreement in March 2009. The executive provided some of the requested documents to the committee and Ms. Miers was permitted to testify, under oath, in a closed, but transcribed hearing.

4. On April 9, and May 5, 2008, the House Oversight and Government Reform Committee issued three subpoenas total to the Administrator of the Environmental Protection Agency (EPA) and the Office of Information and Regulatory Affairs of the Office of Management and Budget (OIRA). The subpoenas sought documents related to EPA's promulgation of regulations serving national ambient air quality standards for ozone on March 12, 2008. Another subpoena requested communications between the EPA and OIRA concerning the agency's decision to deny a petition by California for a waiver from federal preemption to enable the state to regulate greenhouse gas emissions from motor vehicles. On June 19, 2008, the Attorney General advised the President that 25 of the documents covered by the subpoena would be properly covered by an assertion of executive privilege. On June 20, 2008, the EPA Administrator advised the Chairman of the Committee that he had been directed by the President to assert executive privilege with respect to the withheld documents. The committee did not pursue a contempt action.
5. Removal and Replacement of U.S. Attorneys (2008). On July 10, 2008, Karl Rove, a former White House Deputy Chief of Staff, refused to comply with a subpoena requiring his appearance before the House Judiciary Committee's Subcommittee on Commercial and Administrative Law, claiming absolute immunity on the basis of White House and DOJ opinions and directions. By a vote of 7-1, the Subcommittee rejected his claims of privilege. On July 30, 2008, the full Judiciary Committee approved a report recommending that Mr. Rove be cited for contempt by the House. The full House never voted on the contempt citation. Mr. Rove was permitted to testify as part of the accommodation reached between the executive and the House at the conclusion of the Miers/Bolten dispute discussed above.
6. Special Counsel's Investigation of Revelations of CIA Agent's Identity. On July 16, 2008, the President directed the Attorney General (at the behest of the Attorney General) to assert executive privilege with respect to a House Oversight and Government Reform Committee subpoena to the DOJ. The subpoena concerned DOJ's investigation by a Special Counsel of the public revelation of Valerie Plame Wilson's identity as an employee of the Central Intelligence Agency. The documents sought and withheld included FBI reports of the Special Counsel's interviews with the Vice President and senior White House staff, handwritten notes taken by the Deputy National

Security Advisor during conversations with the Vice President and senior White House officials, and other documents provided by the White House during the course of the investigation. The Attorney General requested that the President formally assert the privilege after the Committee scheduled a meeting to consider a resolution citing him for contempt of Congress. The Chairman of the Oversight Committee delayed a scheduled committee vote on contempt to allow Members to assess the executive privilege assertion. The Committee later requested a privilege log but neither the DOJ nor the White House responded to that request.

9. Obama

President Obama has only formally invoked executive privilege once, in relation to a congressional investigation of Operation Fast and Furious. At the direction of the President, on June 20, 2012, Deputy Attorney General James Cole informed the House Committee on Oversight and Government Reform that the President was formally asserting executive privilege over documents requested pursuant to a subpoena issued as part of the Committee's investigation of Operation Fast and Furious. A letter from the Attorney General to the President, dated June 19, 2012, laid out the executive's legal argument for asserting the privilege. The Attorney General argued that the documents withheld included internal executive branch communications generated in the course of deliberative process concerning responses to congressional oversight. Furthermore, he stated that executive privilege encompasses executive branch deliberative communications and that disclosing such documents would "inhibit the candor of such Executive Branch deliberations ... " Letter to the President from Attorney General Eric Holder, June 19, 2012. On June 20, 2012, the Committee voted to hold Attorney General Eric Holder, the subject of the subpoena as custodian of DOJ documents, in contempt of Congress. The full House voted in favor of a criminal contempt citation on June 28, 2012. The House Committee on Oversight and Government Reform filed a civil lawsuit in the U.S. District Court for the District of Columbia on August 13, 2012, seeking to enforce the subpoena and compel disclosure of the documents being withheld due to the assertion of executive privilege.

End Notes

[1] See Archibald Cox, Executive Privilege, 122 U. PA. L. REV. 1383, 1395-1405 (1979). See generally Mark J. Rozell, EXECUTIVE PRIVILEGE: PRESIDENTIAL POWERS, SECRECY, AND ACCOUNTABILITY, (2d ed., rev. 2002) [hereinafter Rozell, PRESIDENTIAL POWERS); Mark J. Rozell, Executive Privilege and Modern Presidents: In Nixon's Shadow, 83 MINN. L. REV. 1069 (1999) [hereinafter Rozell, Modern Presidents].

[2] See Neil Devins, Congressional-Executive Information Access Disputes: A Modest Proposal-Do Nothing, 48 ADM. L. REV. 109 (1996).

[3] United States v. AT&T, 551 F.2d 384 (D.C. Cir. 1976) [hereinafter AT&T I]; Senate Select Comm. on Presidential Campaign Activities v. Nixon, 498 F.2d 725 (D.C. Cir. 1974) [hereinafter Senate Select Comm.]; Comm. on the Judiciary v. Miers, 558 F. Supp. 2d 53 (D.D.C. 2008); United States v. House of Representatives, 556 F. Supp. 150 (D.D.C. 1983).

[4] Senate Select Comm., 498 F.2d 725; Miers, 558 F. Supp. 2d 53.

[5] 121 F.3d 729 (D.C. Cir. 1997).

[6] 365 F.3d 1108 (D.C. Cir. 2004).

[7] However, it is important to note that these cases did not arise in a congressional-executive dispute context, but rather out of a grand jury subpoena and a FOIA request, respectively.

[8] See generally Miers, 558 F. Supp. 2d 53.

[9] Id. at 100-07.

[10] 487 F.2d 750 (D.C. Cir. 1973).

[11] Id. at 757.

[12] Id.

[13] 498 F.2d 725 (D.C. Cir. 1974).

[14] Id. 730-31.

[15] Id. at 731.

[16] Id. at 732 (emphasis supplied).

[17] Id. (emphasis supplied).

[18] Id. at 733.

[19] Senate Select Comm., 498 F.2d at 733.

[20] This reading of Senate Select Committee was a persistent characteristic of the statements of the Reagan, George H.W. Bush and Clinton Administrations. See, e.g., Letter from Attorney General William French Smith to President Reagan, October 31, 1981, reprinted in 5 Op. O.L.C. 27, 30 (1981) [hereinafter Smith Letter/Watt]; Memorandum to General Counsels' Consultative Group Re: Congressional Requests for Confidential Executive Branch Information, 13 Op. O.L.C. 153, 157 (1989) [hereinafter Barr Memo]; Letter from Attorney General Janet Reno to President Clinton, September 20, 1996, at 2-3 [hereinafter Reno Letter/Haiti]; Letter from Attorney General Janet Reno to President Clinton, September 16, 1999 [hereinafter Reno Letter/FALN]. It is utilized in buttressing President George W. Bush's June 28, 2007, privilege claim with respect to demands for documents and testimony sought by the House and Senate Judiciary Committees relating to their investigations concerning the dismissal and replacement of nine U.S. Attorneys. See also Appendix, "Bush, George W.".

[21] Senate Select Comm., 498 F.2d at 731.

[22] Id. at 732-33.

[23] Id. at 733. It is important to note that the Select Committee was established by Senate Resolution 60 as a special investigation committee with no legislative authority. Its sole

mission was to determine the facts about the Watergate break-in and its aftermath and report to the Senate its findings and recommendations. S.Res. 60, 93rd Cong. (1973).

[24] 2 The Records of the Constitutional Convention of 1787, at 206 (Max Farrand, ed., 1966).

[25] Woodrow Wilson, Congressional Government 195, 198 (Meridian Books 1956) (1885).

[26] See, e.g., Hutchinson v. Proxmire, 443 U.S. 111, 132 (1979).

[27] Watkins v. United States, 354 U.S. 173, 187 (1957). See also McGrain v. Daugherty, 273 U.S. 135, 177 (1926); Eastland v. U.S. Servicemen's Fund, 421 U.S. 491, 504 n.15 (1975).

[28] 418 U.S. 683 (1974) [hereinafter Nixon I].

[29] Id. at 705-06, 708, 711.

[30] Id. at 705-06, 708.

[31] Id. at 706.

[32] Id.

[33] Id. at 707.

[34] Nixon I, 418 U.S. at 713.

[35] Id. at 712 n.19.

[36] 433 U.S. 425 (1977) [hereinafter Nixon II].

[37] P.L. 93-526, 88 Stat. 1695 (1974).

[38] Nixon II, 433 U.S. at 439.

[39] Id. at 446.

[40] Id. at 449 (internal citations omitted).

[41] Id. at 453.

[42] 567 F.2d 121 (D.C. Cir. 1977) [hereinafter AT&T II].

[43] This was the second time the case was before the court. After its initial review it was remanded to the district court to allow the parties further opportunity to negotiate an accommodation. See AT&T I, 551 F.2d 384.

[44] AT&T II, 567 F.2d at 127 n.17.

[45] Id. at 128.

[46] Id.

[47] Id. at 129.

[48] Id. at 127-28.

[49] Id. at 127 (internal citations omitted).

[50] AT&T II, 567 F.2d at 130.

[51] Id. at 123, 126.

[52] Id. at 131-32.

[53] 556 F. Supp. 150 (D.D.C. 1983).

[54] Id. at 151.

[55] Id. at 152-53.

[56] Id. at 152, 153.

[57] See Devins, supra, note 2, at 118-20.

[58] See Memorandum for the Attorney General Re: Confidentiality of the Attorney General's Communications in Counseling the President, 6 Op. O.L.C. 481, 484-90 (1982) [hereinafter Olson Memo]; Barr Memo, supra note 20, at 154.

[59] See Smith Letter/Watt, supra note 20, at 28-31; Barr Memo, supra note 20, at 187-90; Reno Letter/FALN, supra note 20.

[60] See, e.g., Nixon I, 418 U.S. at 705. See also Smith Letter/Watt, supra note 20, at 29; Memorandum for All Executive Department and Agency General Counsel's Re: Congressional Requests to Departments and Agencies Protected By Executive Privilege, September 28, 1994, at 1, 2 [hereinafter Cutler Memo]; Letter from Jack Quinn to Hon.

William A. Zellif, Jr., October 1, 1996, at 1 [hereinafter Quinn Letter/FBI]; Memorandum from President Bush to Secretary of Defense Richard Cheney Re: Congressional Subpoena for an Executive Branch Document, August 8, 1991, at 1 [hereinafter Bush Memo].

[61] Smith Letter/Watt, supra note 20, at 31; accord Barr Memo, supra note 20, at 192 ("Congress will seldom have any legitimate legislative interest in knowing the precise predecisional positions and statements of particular Executive Branch officials."); Letter from Assistant Attorney General Robert Rabkin, Office of Legislative Affairs, DOJ, to Honorable John Linder, Chairman House Subcommittee on Rules and Organization of the House, Committee on Rules, June 27, 2000 at 5-6 ("[T]he Department has a broad confidentiality interest in matters that reflect its internal deliberative process. In particular, we have sought to ensure that all law enforcement and litigation decisions are products of open, frank, and independent assessments of the law and facts—uninhibited by political and improper influences that may be present outside the department. We have long been concerned about the chilling effect that would ripple throughout government if prosecutors, policy advisors at all levels and line attorneys believed that their honest opinion—be it 'good' or 'bad' - may be the topic of debate in Congressional hearings or floor debates. These include assessments of evidence and law, candid advice on strength and weaknesses of legal arguments, and recommendations to take or not to take legal action against individuals and corporate entities.") [hereinafter Rabkin Letter]; see also Smith Letter/Watt, supra note 20, at 30 ("congressional oversight interest will support a demand for predecisional, deliberative documents in the possession of the Executive Branch only in the most unusual circumstances").

[62] Smith Letter/Watt, supra note 20, at 30; see also Statement of Assistant Attorney General William H. Rehnquist, reprinted in Executive Privilege: The Withholding of Information by the Executive: Hearings Before the Subcommittee on Separation of Powers of the Senate Committee on the Judiciary, 92nd Cong., 1st Sess. 424 ("The notion that the advisors whom he has chosen should bear some sort of a hybrid responsibility to opinion makers outside of the government, which notion in practice would inevitably have the effect of diluting their responsibility to him, is entirely inconsistent with our tripartite systems of government. The President is entitled to undivided and faithful advice from his subordinates, just as Senators and Representatives are entitled to the same sort of advice from their legislative and administrative assistants, and judges to the same sort of advice from their law clerks.") [hereinafter Rehnquist Statement]; Rabkin Letter, supra note 61 ("The foregoing concerns apply with special force to Congressional requests for prosecution and declination memoranda and similar documents. These are extremely sensitive law enforcement materials. The Department's attorneys are asked to render unbiased, professional judgments about the merits of potential criminal and civil law enforcement cases. If their deliberative documents were made subject to Congressional challenge and scrutiny, we would face a grave danger that they would be chilled from providing the candid and independent analysis essential to just and effective law enforcement or just as troubling, that our assessments of the strengths and weaknesses of evidence of the law, before they are presented in court. That may result in an unfair advantage to those who seek public funds and deprive the taxpayers of confidential representation enjoyed by other litigants.").

[63] Smith Letter/Watt, supra note 20, at 29.

[64] See Rozell, supra note 1, at 39-40.

[65] In his prepared statement to the Subcommittee on Separation of Powers of the Senate Judiciary Committee, Assistant Attorney General Rehnquist distinguished between "those few executive branch witnesses whose sole responsibility is that of advising the President" who

"should not be required to appear [before Congress] at all, since all of their official responsibilities would be subject to a claim of privilege" and "the executive branch witness ... whose responsibilities include the administration of departments or agencies established by Congress, and from whom Congress may quite properly require extensive testimony," subject to "appropriate" claims of privilege. Rehnquist Statement, supra note 62, at 427. Moreover, in colloquy with Senator Ervin, Mr. Rehnquist seemed to accept that the privilege protected only communications with some nexus to presidential decision making: SENATOR ERVIN: As I construe your testimony, the decisionmaking process category would apply to communications between presidential advisers and the President and also to communications made between subordinates of the President when they are engaged in the process of determining what recommendations they should make to the President in respect to matters of policy. MR. REHNQUIST: It would certainly extend that far, yes. Id. at 439-40. See also Rozell, supra note 1, at 65-66.

[66] See Olson Memo, supra note 58, at 489.

[67] Bush Memo, supra note 60, at 1; Letter from General Counsel, DOD, Terrence O'Donnell to Hon. John Conyers, Jr., October 8, 1991, at 5 [hereinafter O'Donnell Letter].

[68] See, e.g., Cutler Memo, supra note 60, at 2.

[69] See, e.g., id. (Communications between White House and departments or agencies, including advice to or from to White House); Reno Letter/FALN, supra note 20.

[70] See CRS Report RL33667, Presidential Signing Statements: Constitutional and Institutional Implications, by Todd Garvey.

[71] See, e.g., Executive Order 13233 issued by President Bush on November 1, 2001, which gave current and former Presidents and Vice Presidents broad authority to withhold presidential records and delay their release indefinitely. It vests former Vice Presidents, and the heirs or designees of disabled or deceased presidents the authority to assert executive privilege, and expands the scope of claims of privilege. Hearings held by the House Committee on Government Reform in 2002 raised substantial questions as to the constitutionality of the Order and resulted in the reporting of legislation (H.R. 4187) in the 107th Congress that would have nullified the Order and established new processes for presidential claims of privilege and for congressional and public access to presidential records. H.Rept. 107-790, 107th Cong. 2nd Sess. (2002). Substantially the same legislation (H.R. 1225) passed the House on March 14, 2007. See H.Rept. 110-44, 110th Cong. 1st Sess. (2007), and was reported out of the Senate Committee on Homeland Security and Governmental Affairs on June 20, 2007, without amendment and with no written report. See generally, Jonathan Turley, Presidential Papers and Popular Government: The Convergence of Constitutional and Property Theory in Claims of Ownership and Control of Presidential Records, 88 CORNELL L. REV. 651, 666-96 (2003).

[72] See Letter dated May 21, 2004 to Hon. Alex M. Azar, II, General Counsel, Department of Health and Human Services from Jack L. Goldsmith III, Assistant Attorney General, Office of Legal Counsel, Department of Justice, available at, http://www.usdoj.gov/olc/crsmemoresponsese.htm [hereinafter Azar Letter]. This broad view of presidential privilege was repeated in Attorney General Mukasey's request to the President that he claim executive privilege with respect to a House Committee subpoena for DOJ documents in an investigation by a DOJ Special Counsel in the revelation of a CIA agent's identity. See Letter to the President from Attorney General Mukasey, dated July 15, 2008. See also Appendix, "Bush, George W.".

[73] Azar Letter at 3.

[74] Exec. Order No. 13489 (Jan. 21, 2009) (revoking Exec. Order No. 13233 (Nov. 1, 2001)).

[75] Id.

[76] See, CRS Report RL33667, Presidential Signing Statements: Constitutional and Institutional Implications, by Todd Garvey.

[77] See, Statement of President Barack Obama Upon Signing H.R. 1105, March 11, 2009 (objecting to §714(1) and §714(2)); Statement of President Barack Obama Upon Signing S. 386, May 20, 2009 (objecting to §5(d)); Statement of President Barack Obama Upon Signing H.R. 2701, October 7, 2010 (objecting to §331 and §405); Statement of President Barack Obama Upon Signing H.R. 1473, April 15, 2011 (objecting to §2262).

[78] Cutler Memo, supra note 59, at 1.

[79] Congressional Subpoenas of Department of Justice Investigative Files, 8 Op. O.L.C. 315 (1984). Accord Assertion of Executive Privilege in Response to Congressional Demands for Law Enforcement Files, 6 Op. O.L.C. 31, 36 (1982) ("These principles will not be employed to shield documents which contain evidence of criminal or unethical conduct by agency officials from proper review.") [hereinafter Smith Letter/EPA].

[80] See David Hoffman, President Offers to Share Iran Sales Notes with Hill; Aides Reversed on Memoir Materials, WASH. POST, Feb. 3, 1987, at A1.

[81] Olson Memo, supra note 58, at 486; Rabkin Letter, supra note 61.

[82] Id. But see Smith Letter/EPA, supra note 79, at 32 ("policy does not extend to all material contained in investigative files.... The only documents which have been withheld are those which are sensitive memoranda or notes by ... attorneys and investigators reflecting enforcement strategy, legal analysis, lists of potential witnesses, settlement considerations, and similar materials the disclosure of which might adversely affect a pending enforcement action, overall enforcement policy, or the rights of individuals").

[83] Cutler Memo, supra note 60, at 1; accord Memorandum from President Reagan for the Heads of Executive Departments, and Agencies Re: Procedures for Governing Responses to Congressional Requests for Information, November 4, 1982 [hereinafter Reagan Memo]; Rabkin Letter, supra note 61, at 1-2

[84] Cutler Memo, supra note 60, at 1.

[85] Reagan Memo, supra note 83, at 1.

[86] Barr Memo, supra note 20, at 185.

[87] Id. at 185, 186; see Rozell, supra note 1, at 106-08.

[88] Rehnquist Statement, supra note 62, at 420.

[89] Smith Letter/Watt, supra note 20, at 31.

[90] Reagan Memo, supra note 83, at 1.

[91] Rehnquist Statement, supra note 62, at 422.

[92] Id.

[93] Letter from Attorney General Janet Reno to President Clinton, September 20, 1996, at 2-3 [hereinafter Reno Letter/Haiti]; Letter from Attorney General Reno to President Clinton, September 30, 1996, at 2 [hereinafter Reno Letter/FBI]; Letter from Attorney General Reno to President Clinton, September 16, 1999 [hereinafter Reno Letter/FALN]. The Acting Attorney General's opinion accompanying President George W. Bush's June 28, 2007, claim of executive privilege, discussed in infra at 24-26, relies heavily on the Senate Select Committee precedent.

[94] 498 F.2d at 731.

[95] See, infra, "President Obama's Assertion of Executive Privilege"

[96] Letter to President Barack Obama, from Eric Holder, Attorney General, June 19, 2012 at 3.

[97] Id.

[98] Reagan Memo, supra note 71, at 2.

[99] Cutler Memo, supra note 20, at 2-3.

[100] See the Appendix of this Report for a compilation of executive privilege claims from the Kennedy through the Obama Administrations.

[101] Clinton v. Jones, 520 U.S. 681 (1997) (no temporary presidential immunity from civil suit for unofficial acts); In re Grand Jury Subpoena Duces Tecum, 112 F.3d 910 (8th Cir. 1997), cert. denied 521 U.S. 1105 (1997) (claims of attorney-client and work product privilege denied); In re Sealed Case, 121 F.3d 729 (D.C. Cir 1977) (claims of executive privilege rejected) [hereinafter Espy]; In re Sealed Case, 124 F.3d 230 (D.C. Cir. 1997) (claims of attorney-client and work product privilege denied); In re Sealed Case, 148 F.3d 1073 (D.C. Cir. 1998), cert. denied 525 U.S. 990 (1998) (claim of "protective function" privilege denied); In re Bruce R. Lindsey (Grand Jury Testimony), 148 F.3d 1100 (D.C. Cir. 1998) (claims of attorney-client and work product privilege denied).

[102] 121 F.3d 729 (D.C. Cir. 1997).

[103] Id. at 745-46; see also id. at 737-38 ("[W]here there is reason to believe the documents sought may shed light on government misconduct, the [deliberative process] privilege is routinely denied on the grounds that shielding internal government deliberations in this context does not serve 'the public interest in honest, effective government.'").

[104] Id. at 745, 752; see also id. at 753 ("... these communications nonetheless are ultimately connected with presidential decisionmaking").

[105] Id. at 754, 757.

[106] In contrast, the deliberative process privilege does not protect documents that simply state or explain a decision the government has already made or material that is purely factual, unless the material is inextricably intertwined with the deliberative portions of the materials so that disclosure would effectively reveal the deliberations. Id. at 737.

[107] Id. at 745.

[108] Id. at 752.

[109] Espy, 121 F.3d at 752.

[110] Id. (footnote omitted).

[111] Id. at 752.

[112] Id. at 752-53.

[113] See, e.g., Youngstown Sheet & Tube Co. v. Sawyer, 343 U.S. 579, 587 (1952); Myers v. United States, 272 U.S. 52, 177 (1926) (Holmes, J., dissenting); Kendall ex rel. Stokes v. United States, 37 U.S. (12 Pet.) 522, 612-13 (1838); Nat'l Treasury Emps. Union v. Nixon, 492 F.2d 587, 604 (D.C. Cir. 1974).

[114] See Espy, 121 F.3d at 752-53. But cf. Loving v. Dep't of Defense, 550 F.3d 32 (D.C. Cir. 2008) (characterizing the presidential communications privilege as including documents related to "presidential decisionmaking and deliberations," but never mentioning a requirement that the function being exercised be "quintessential and non-delegable").

[115] Espy, 121 F.3d at 748.

[116] Id. at 750.

[117] Id. at 752.

[118] 34 Stat. 225 (1906) (codified as amended at 16 U.S.C. §§ 431-433 (2006)).

[119] 16 U.S.C. § 431 (2006).

[120] See 143 Cong. Rec. E2259-72 (daily ed. Nov. 9, 1997) (statement of Hon. James V. Hansen presenting staff study of committee actions and documents in regard to the establishment of the Grand Staircase-Escalante National Monument); see also Ruth Larson, White House Yields Papers on Utah Wilderness Decision, WASH. TIMES, Oct. 23, 1997, A3. Of course,

the White House action cannot be deemed a concession of the legal argument in the absence of an explanation for its decision to disclose the material.

121 The notion that a congressional delegation of administrative decision-making authority is implicitly a concurrent delegation of authority to the President is effectively countered by Professor Kevin Stack in The President's Statutory Power to Administer the Laws, 106 COLUM. L. REV. 263 (2006).

122 365 F.3d 1108 (D.C. Cir. 2004). The panel split 2-1, with Judge Rogers writing for the majority and Judge Randolph dissenting.

123 The President has delegated the formal process of review and recommendation of his pardon authority to the Attorney General who, in turn, has delegated it to the Deputy Attorney General. The Deputy Attorney General oversees the work of the Office of the Pardon Attorney.

124 Judicial Watch, 365 F.3d at 1109-12.

125 Id. at 1112.

126 Id. at 1114.

127 Id. at 1117.

128 Id. at 1121-22.

129 Judicial Watch, 365 F.3d at 1116.

130 Id. at 1116-17.

131 Id. at 1118-24.

132 Letter dated June 28, 2007 to Chairman Conyers and Leahy from Fred F. Fielding, Counsel to the President, available at http://www.judiciary.senate.gov/resources/documents/upload/110thCongress-2007Documents.pdf.

133 Memorandum, dated June 27, 2007, for the President from Paul D. Clement, Solicitor General and Acting Attorney General, available at http://www.judiciary.senate.gov/resources/documents/upload/110thCongress-2007Documents.pdf [hereinafter Clement Memo].

134 Id. at 1.

135 Id. at 2 (citing Nixon I, 418 U.S. at 708).

136 Id. (citing Espy, 121 F.3d at 752).

137 Id.

138 Memorandum for the Counsel to the President Re: Immunity of Former Counsel to the President from Compelled Congressional Testimony from Principal Deputy Assistant Attorney General, Office Legal Counsel, DOJ, dated July 10, 2007, available at http://www.justice.gov/olc/2007/miers-immunity-Opinion071007.pdf [hereinafter OLC Immunity Opinion].

139 Id. at 1.

140 Id. at 2.

141 See 2 U.S.C. §§ 192, 194 (stating that the President of the Senate or Speaker of the House shall certify the citation to the U.S. Attorney, "whose duty it shall be to bring the matter before the grand jury for its action"). For detailed information about the criminal contempt statutes, see CRS Report RL34097, Congress's Contempt Power and the Enforcement of Congressional Subpoenas: Law, History, Practice, and Procedure, by Todd Garvey and Alissa M. Dolan.

142 H.Rept. 110-423 110th Cong., 1st Sess. (2007).

143 H.Res. 982, 110th Cong. (Feb. 14, 2008). The vote total is low because 173 Members did not vote. According to the Washington Post, "Republicans walked off the floor and refused to cast a final vote." Paul Kane, West Wing Aides Cited for Contempt, WASH. POST, Feb.

15, 2008, available at http://www.washingtonpost.com/wp-dyn/content/article/ 2008/02/14/ AR2008021402415.html.

[144] The House only voted on one resolution, H.Res. 982. However, the text of this resolution stated, "Resolved, That House Resolution 979 and House Resolution 980 are hereby adopted." Therefore, the House only recorded one vote, but voted in favor of passing two resolutions.

145 H.Res. 979, 110th Cong. (Feb. 14, 2008).

[146] Letter from Attorney General Michael Mukasey to Speaker of the House Nancy Pelosi, Feb. 29, 2008 (on file with the authors).

[147] Complaint for Declaratory and Injunctive Relief, Comm. on the Judiciary, U.S. House of Representative v. Miers, 558 F. Supp. 2d 53 (D.D.C. 2008) (No. 08-0409).

[148] Id. at 10-11.

[149] Plaintiff's Motion for Partial Summary Judgment at 1-2, Comm. on the Judiciary, U.S. House of Representative v. Miers, 558 F. Supp. 2d 53 (D.D.C. 2008) (No. 08-0409).

[150] Memorandum of Points and Authorities in Support of Defendants' Motion to Dismiss and in Opposition to Plaintiff's Motion for Partial Summary Judgment on Counts I and II at 5-8, U.S. House of Representative v. Miers, 558 F. Supp. 2d 53 (D.D.C. 2008) (No. 08-0409).

[151] Id. at 8-9.

[152] The court declined to order Ms. Miers and Mr. Bolten to provide detailed privilege logs for documents claimed to be covered by executive privilege, holding that while such logs "have great practical utility," there is no applicable statute or controlling case law that would provide "a ready ground by which to force the Executive to make such a production strictly in response to a congressional subpoena." Miers, 558 F. Supp. 2d at 107 (emphasis in original). The court warned, however, that both the court "and the parties will need some way to evaluate privilege assertions going forward in the context of this litigation." Id. The court particularly noted that if it has to decide the merits of a privilege claim, the government "will need a better description of the documents than the one found in Mr. Clement's letter of June 27, 2007." See Clement Memo, supra notes 127-37 and accompanying text. With this admonition, the court ordered that the defendants "shall provide to the plaintiff a specific description of any documents withheld from production on the basis of executive privilege consistent with the terms of the Memorandum Opinion issued on this date." Order at 1-2, Comm. on the Judiciary, U.S. House of Representatives v. Miers, 558 F. Supp. 2d 53 (D.D.C. 2008).

[153] Miers, 558 F. Supp. 2d at 75 (citing McGrain, 273 U.S. at 174).

[154] Id. (citing Eastland, 421 U.S. at 505).

[155] Id. at 99 (citing Response to Congressional Requests for Information Regarding Decisions Made Under the Independent Counsel Act, 10 Op. O.L.C. 68 (1986) [hereinafter Cooper Memo]).

[156] Id. For an in-depth discussion of the implications and importance of the court's justiciability rulings, see CRS Report RL34097, Congress's Contempt Power and the Enforcement of Congressional Subpoenas: Law, History, Practice, and Procedure, by Todd Garvey and Alissa M. Dolan.

[157] Miers, 558 F. Supp. 2d at 99.

[158] 339 U.S. 323 (1950).

[159] Id. at 331.

[160] 457 U.S. 800 (1982).

[161] Id. at 808.

[162] Id. at 807.

[163] Id. at 810.
[164] Id. at 812-13.
[165] Miers, 558 F. Supp. 2d at 100-01, 104-05.
[166] Id. at 102 (emphasis in original) (internal citations omitted).
[167] Nixon I, 418 U.S. at 707-08.
[168] Miers, 558 F. Supp. 2d at 102-03.
[169] Id. at 103-04.
[170] Id. at 105.
[171] Committee on the Judiciary v. Miers, 542 F.3d 909 (D.C. Cir. 2008) [hereinafter Miers II].
[172] Id. at 911. The authority underlying a House subpoena or contempt citation has traditionally been considered to expire at the termination of the Congress in which it was authorized.
[173] The concurring opinion appeared to disagree with the majority on this point, arguing that "the successor Congress can assert the prior Committee's investigatory interest..." Committee on the Judiciary v. Miers, 542 F.3d 909, 912 (D.C. Cir. 2008) (Tatel, Judge, concurring) (citing United States v. AT&T Co., 567 F.2d 121 (D.C. Cir. 1977)).
[174] Presidential Records Act, 44 U.S.C. §§2201-2207.
[175] Committee on the Judiciary v. Miers, 2009 U.S. Dist. LEXIS 2326 (D.D.C. 2009).
[176] David Johnston, Top Bush Aides to Testify in Attorneys' Firings, N.Y. TIMES, March. 4, 2009. The settlement also permitted Karl Rove to testify under the same conditions.
[177] Committee on the Judiciary v. Miers, 2009 U.S. App. LEXIS 29374 (D.C. Cir. 2009).
[178] The testimony and documents are available at http://judiciary.house.gov/issues/issues_WHInterviews.html.: http://judiciary.house.gov/issues/issues_WHInterviews.html.
[179] Miers, 558 F. Supp. 2d. at 105.
[180] Id. at 101, 106.
[181] 550 F.3d 32 (D.C. Cir. 2008).
[182] Id. at 37.
[183] Id. ("[T]wo executive privileges [] are relevant here: the presidential communications privilege and the deliberative process privilege.").
[184] Id. at 39.
[185] Id. at 40 ("Nothing in Judicial Watch disturbs the established principle that communications 'directly involving' the President ...are entitled to the privilege, regardless of whether the President solicited them."). In addition, the Loving opinion reaffirmed that the presidential communications privilege "is more difficult to surmount' than the deliberative process privilege, and that the presidential communications privilege protects a documents in its entirety, whereas under the deliberative process privilege the government must "segregate and disclose non-privileged factual information within a document." Id. at 38-40.
[186] For a detailed discussion of Operation Fast and Furious, see CRS Report RL32842, Gun Control Legislation, by William J. Krouse.
[187] A "straw purchase" occurs when an individual poses as the actual transferee, but he is actually acquiring the firearm for another person. In effect, he serves as an illegal middleman.
[188] James V. Grimaldi and Sari Horwitz, ATF Probe Strategy is Questioned, WASH. POST, Feb. 2, 2011, at A4.
[189] "Gun walking" refers to guns that were trafficked to gunrunners and other criminals before ATF moved to arrest the suspects and seize all of their contraband firearms. See id.
[190] Grimaldi and Horwitz, supra note 188, at A4.
[191] John Solomon, David Heath, and Gordon Witkin, "ATF Let Hundred of U.S. Weapons Fall into Hands of Suspected Mexican Gun Runners: Whistleblower Says Agents Strongly Objected to Risky Strategy," Center for Public Integrity, available at

http://www.iwatchnews.org/2011/03/03/2095/atf-let-hundreds-us-weapons-fall-hands-suspected- mexicangunrunners.

[192] Pete Yost, Justice IG to Look into Anti-Gun Efforts on Border, ASSOCIATED PRESS ONLINE, March 4, 2011.

[193] Letter from Assistant Attorney General Ronald Weich to Ranking Member Charles Grassley, February 4, 2011, available at http://oversight.house.gov/wp-content/uploads/2012/06/Feb-4-Dec-2-letters.pdf.

[194] Report of the Committee on Oversight and Government Reform U.S. House of Representatives, "Report Recommending that the House of Representatives Find Eric H. Holder, Jr., Attorney General, U.S. Department of Justice in Contempt of Congress for Refusal to Comply With a Subpoena Duly Issued by the Committee on Oversight and Government Reform, June 20, 2012, p. 4 [hereinafter Contempt Committee Report].

[195] Press Release, "Chairman Issa Subpoenas ATF for 'Project Gunrunner' Documents," April 1, 2011.

[196] The Committee hearings included: June 13, 2011: "Obstruction of Justice: Does the Justice Department Have to Respond to a Lawfully Issued and Valid Congressional Subpoena?"; June 15, 2011: "Operation Fast and Furious: Reckless Decisions, Tragic Outcomes"; July 26, 2011: "Operation Fast and Furious: The Other Side of the Border"; February 2, 2012: "Fast and Furious: Management Failures at the Department of Justice" (Attorney General Holder testified); June 20, 2012: "Full Committee Business Meeting" (voting on citation to hold Attorney General Holder in contempt).

[197] Jerry Jarkon, Holder Amends Remarks on Gun Sting: Attorney General Heard of 'Fast and Furious' Earlier Than He First Said, WASH. POST, Nov. 9, 2011, at A2.

[198] Letter from Deputy Attorney General James Cole to Chairman Darrell Issa and Ranking Member Charles Grassley, December 2, 2011, available at http://oversight.house.gov/wp-content/uploads/2012/06/Feb-4-Dec-2-letters.pdf.

[199] Id.

[200] Id.

[201] Letter from Deputy Attorney General James Cole to Chairman Darrell Issa, June 20, 2012, available at http://i2.cdn.turner.com/cnn/2012/images/06/20/letter_to_issa.pdf [hereinafter June 20 Letter]

[202] Id.

[203] Contempt Committee Report, p. 22.

[204] Id. at 4.

[205] Congressional Quarterly Hearing Transcript: "House Oversight and Government Reform Committee Holds Markup on a Contempt of Congress Citation for U.S. Attorney General Holder," available at http://www.cq.com/doc/ congressionaltranscripts-4110610 [hereinafter Hearing Transcript].

[206] Id.

[207] Contempt Committee Report, p. i.

[208] June 20 Letter.

[209] Id.

[210] Contempt Committee Report, p. 42 (as stated in Representative Gowdy's amendment, approved by a 23 to 17 vote).

[211] Ed O'Keefe and Sari Horwitz, Fast and Furious: House Committee Votes 23-17 to Hold Attorney General Eric Holder in Contempt of Congress, WASH. POST, June 20, 2011, available at http://www.washingtonpost.com/blogs/ 2chambers/post/live-fast-and-furious-

hearing-to-discuss-contempt-of-congress-charge-against-eric-holder/2012/06/20/gJQAzQKHqV_blog.html.

[212] See H.Res. 711 (roll call vote available at http://cq.com/doc/floorvote-236138000). For detailed information on the contempt process, see CRS Report RL34097, Congress's Contempt Power and the Enforcement of Congressional Subpoenas: Law, History, Practice, and Procedure, by Todd Garvey and Alissa M. Dolan.

[213] Miers, 558 F. Supp. 2d at 103.

[214] Espy, 121 F.3d at 753.

Index

D

E

F

G

Q

R

S

T

U

V

W